The Art of Virtue

PAUL CHARA

WINEPRESS WP PUBLISHING

ISBN 1-57921-189-5
Library of Congress Catalog Card Number: 99-66105

To order additional copies of

The Art
of Virtue

send $19.95 plus $3.95 shipping and handling to

Books Etc.
PO Box 4888
Seattle, WA 98104

or have your credit card ready and call

(800) 917-BOOK

Contents

Wisdom has built her house.
She has hewn out and
set up her seven pillars.

—Proverbs 9:1

Acknowledgements

To my parents, Paul and Linnie Chara, for teaching me courage: You taught me to dare to fail.

To Timothy Botts for demonstrating justice: You graciously gave of your artistic talent (the calligraphy was just beautiful) to help a struggling author.

To Janet Hamm, Chip McGregor, and Bill Watkins for the wisdom of your words and editing. The hardest words to hear are often the most instructive.

To Christian, Karston, Kristof, Symon, and Seth for teaching me the value of temperance. The fruit of self-control is always shared by others.

To Pastor Gary Kirst for your faith in me. The opportunity to teach virtue was the seed that led to this book.

To Judie Harron and Athena Dean for encouraging me to hope. It's easier to look forward to the future when you have people helping you in the present.

To the love of God and my wife, Kathleen: You love me!

Thanks also to the following for the privilege of reprinting poems in this book:

- Harcourt Brace Jovanovich for permission to reprint "Upstream" by Carl Sanburg.
- Henry Holt and Company for permission to reprint "Stopping by Woods on a Snowy Evening" and "The Road Not Taken" by Robert Frost.
- Yale University Press for permission to reprint "Exit God" by Gamaliel Bradford.

Chapter 1

Adult Lessons from a Child's Story

My mother has always been an avid reader. As a young child she would charm me with stories about her youth, particularly tales about cuddling up on a cold, snowy, wintry night with a favorite book under a flickering light. In my mind's eye I would picture her in a snow-capped, white house in a Norman Rockwell type of setting with one upper room dimly lit. Through the curtains of that room I'd see my mom as a little girl curled up on a bed reading a favorite book. Not surprisingly, that little girl grew up to be a mother who loved to read to her children. And read to me she did. My childhood was filled with stories of brave tin soldiers, talking animals, magical adventures and, most important to me, the *Little Engine That Could*. I grew up to become a professor, and I eventually married a woman (more wonderful than any that could be found in a fairy tale) who loved to read. We usually teach what we are taught, so it is only natural that my wife, Kathleen, and I make it a priority to read frequently to our children.

I tell my Developmental Psychology students that the single most important activity they can do for their children's intellectual development is to read to them, early—starting in the womb—and often. My personal experience and understanding of the research has convinced me that such a practice will yield a bountiful intellectual harvest. While I know that children who are nurtured with books learn great lessons about learning, it was not until a few years ago that it fully struck me how much I, as an adult, learn from reading to my children. Truly, the greatest truths about life are often the simplest ones, and sometimes it is through the simple words of a child's book where the greatest wisdom about living is found. Just such a revelation occurred to me when I was reading the story of an American icon, John Henry, to my children for the first time.* Near the end of the story John Henry dies, and out of the midst of the soft crying of those mourning him a still small voice says: "Dying ain't important. Everybody does that. What matters is how well you do your living." Those words jumped right off the page and into my heart and have been ringing there ever since. Those simple words started me on a journey that I would like to share with you.

"Dying ain't important. Everybody does that. What matters is how well you do your living." It is obvious from the story that those words are spoken of in reference to John Henry. Clearly to those standing around, John Henry had lived well. But what was it about his life that made it so good? To find those clues toward living well, we must go back to the beginning of John Henry's life.

When John Henry was born, it was clear that he was no ordinary child. Knowing that something wonderful was about to happen, the animals of the forest came to greet this extraordinary child born in an ordinary log cabin. And happen it did. John Henry grew into a tall, strong man the first day of life, and sunrise the next day he went to work chopping down trees and splitting logs. Now that's your typical American tale: bigger than life and working hard! Or maybe that used to be the American story. In my younger years I frequently heard about "Yankee ingenuity," and my parents taught me that "Made in America" was synonymous with quality. By the time I became an adult, expressions like the former seemed to disappear from the American vocabulary, and I regret to say I don't fully believe the latter assertion. Something seems to be lost in the society I grew up in: the value of hard work. But here in the story of John Henry something is found, one of the secrets to living well: It's what you do, your actions. You can talk about the moral life and preach about God, but your actions will usually show others the genuineness of your words. *Living well is doing well* is the moral

---

* As wonderfully retold by Julius Lester (New York: Dial Books, 1994).

of the story. Yet, it is not the whole story. Let me illustrate what I mean with an incident in my life that occurred many years ago.

I was going to college in Bozeman, Montana, and one day I finally got up the nerve to ask another student if she wanted to go to a movie with me. She accepted the invitation, and at the prearranged time I drove up to her dorm, escorted her to my car, let her in, got in myself, started the car, and . . . off to the movie. So far, so good, but not for long—about three feet long! That's how far I got before a tire blew out. "Oh ———," I said, to which she replied she didn't like swearing. After apologizing, I went out to change the tire. The weather was bitter cold, "still and clear" as they say in Montana— which means still snowing and clear up to your hip. As my frozen fingers struggled to get off a lug nut, my tire jack snapped and so did my temper. I went into the car and asked my date if she'd mind walking downtown to the theater. She agreed, and off we went. The conversation wasn't very good; the icicles hanging from my mustache and covering my mouth distorted my speaking. The snow in my date's ears hindered her hearing. We finally reached the warm theater. That was good. The snow and ice that we carried on us into the theater melted, leaving us in puddles. That was bad. Walking back soaking wet to her dorm in weather that would only be considered tolerable on the planet Pluto was even worse. I did not give her a kiss goodnight for fear my lips would fall off. Finally making it back to my dorm, I tried to find something positive in the experience. *Well,* I thought, *at least we didn't get attacked by a polar bear.* (Now that would have really been a date to dismember!) I had lots of good intentions, but things turned out so bad.

That incident reveals the problem with trying to judge if a life is well lived solely by a person's actions. We may try to do what's right and it may turn out wrong. Good people can make bad mistakes. Conversely, bad people can do things that seem so good. For example, during the great depression of the 1930s many people were without jobs and food. One wealthy Chicago man, out of his own resources, opened up soup lines to feed the hungry. What a wonderful act. Must have been a good man to do that, right? Not quite. Ever hear of Al Capone? Ever see the films made of the people eating their soup and being sure to say thanks to that "great guy" Al Capone for his goodwill? Maybe Al Capone's motives were good. Conversely, maybe the acts were designed for self-promotion, or some other less-than-honorable reason. We may never know. That's the problem with making judgments based on actions alone: We may never know what the true reasons behind the acts are. Seemingly unselfish acts can mask selfish ambitions, and generous people may appear to be stingy. To get a fuller picture of living well we must go farther than just actions. Just like with John Henry, there is more of the story that must be told.

After a day of hard work, John Henry gets up the next day to go into town for the first time. There he meets the meanest man in town, Ferret-Faced Freddy. This man is so mean "he cried if he had a nice thought." With a voice that "sounded like bat wings on tombstones," Ferret-Faced Freddy is not your run-of-the-mill pleasant conversationalist. Yet John Henry goes right up to Freddy and offers a challenge: John Henry, on foot, will race Freddy, on his horse, through town. If Freddy wins, John will work hard for him for a full year; if John wins, Freddy will have to be nice for a whole year. Freddy gleefully accepts the challenge, and you know who wins the race when you shortly read about "Frederick the Friendly." Fred's attitude is changed for the better, and that brings out the best in his behavior. Freddy now smiles because he has nice thoughts. At the finish line a valuable lesson is learned: It's not just your actions that are important, it's also your attitude. In other words: *Living well is thinking well.* Actions can be misleading, but once we get into a person's mind, there's the heart of the matter of living well. Or is it?

Just as the heart is thought of as the "source" of the lifeblood of the body, so too the mind is thought to be the originator of thinking—the "lifeblood" of consciousness. But where do the contents of thought come from? While the human brain certainly predisposes us to think in certain ways, the primary source of the contents of thought—our beliefs, opinions, feelings, etc.—is the world around us, particularly other people. That's where a major problem comes in. Thinking *well* is usually considered to be so when enough other people agree that it is good or right thinking. Therefore, what everybody thinks or does becomes the norm, and the pressure to fit in leads people to adopt the values of the majority as the voices of their own supposed consciences (that sense of right and wrong, the idea of the way things should be). This becomes even more of a problem as a society becomes dominated by mass communication. The explosion of information leads to an implosion (collapse) of personal standards. This tendency has become clear to me in my years of college teaching.

When historians examine social trends of the twentieth century, they will find a significant one in the content of movies and television programs: The frequency of graphic portrayals of sexual situations involving unmarried couples dramatically increased during this era. How does this impact the viewers of such fare? I see the effects of this every time I cover the topic of premarital sexual intercourse in my Developmental Psychology class. When I come to this topic, I typically have students come up with as many reasons as they can for and against engaging in sex before marriage. In spite of the fact that most students have or will engage in this act, the frequency and the seriousness of the reasons against this behavior always outnumber and outweigh the reasons in favor of it. What surprises me is that even though I teach at a church-affiliated college, reasons based on moral or spiritual standards are rarely brought up in the initial discussion. Furthermore, only a minority of the students report that they have carefully weighed the pros and cons of engaging in sex out of marriage. Considering that sex is a life- (babies are conceived) and-death (abortion, deadly sexually transmitted diseases) act, those are significant omissions in many students' thinking. Could it be that the flood of media information in favor of sex out of marriage has reduced to a trickle students' felt need to examine the acceptability of this behavior from a moral and spiritual perspective? It seems as if the more people are inundated with information, the less effort they put to critically evaluating it, and the more they are at the mercy of those people putting out that message. Why follow an "inner light" if so many others are there to show you the way?

To truly think well, however, we must go beyond what everybody else thinks and what the mass media promote. The focus of thinking well must be transferred from those external sources to a well-reasoned, highly informed internal basis. We must travel down the road of self-examination and make our own way rather than living the ways of others. That's what happens in John Henry's life when he decides to leave home and make his own way in life.

John Henry leaves home, and his father gives him two twenty-pound sledgehammers, telling him, "You've got to have something to make your way in the world with, Son." That's quite instructive: Making your own way is not leaving everything behind. You need to take something with you. The older I get, the more I appreciate what my parents gave me. John Henry takes the hammers, goes down the road, and meets a road crew that has been working hard until they came to a boulder so big that "it took a half a week for a tall man to walk from one side to the other." That's what's going to happen when you go down the road of life: Obstacles are going to show up. When the road crew's efforts to dislodge the boulder by dynamite fail, John Henry lends a hand—or two, to be precise—despite being initially rejected by the crew. John Henry puts his sledgehammers to work and attacks that boulder with so much fury that the dust obscures John Henry from the view of the crew. That's what I like about John Henry: He doesn't retreat from problems, he attacks them heart and soul. Facing the problem and not turning back is what is going to get a person through the problem. Eventually the dust settles, the boulder is gone, and John Henry has made a straight road right through where the boulder once stood. Now we've come to the secret of living well: *Don't base what you think and do on others; make your own way in life.* John Henry did more than take "the road less traveled," he made his own way. But how do I know my own way is the right way? Several years ago at dinner with a woman, I learned just how much of a problem this can be.

My companion and I were having dinner at a nice restaurant when I directed the conversation to her counseling practice. Knowing that she had some unusual techniques, I asked her to describe a case and how she handled it. She then began to tell me, matter-of-factly, about a client who came to her who had been ritualistically sexually abused by her grandparents in a satanic ceremony. I put down my chicken breast after hearing this mouthful. Regaining my composure, I asked her what she told her client. "You need to take responsibility for what happened to you" was my dinner partner's reply.

Thinking that perhaps my brain had short-circuited for a moment and that I misunderstood what she had to say, I asked her to clarify what she meant. I was told that what had happened to this client happened for a reason and the client needed to accept it. As I began to figure out what she meant, and at the same time decide where to get some Alka Seltzer, I inquired if she was talking about bad karma, past lives, reincarnation, and that sort of stuff. Yes, was her reply. Well, I was about to get into some bad karma of my own, let alone the Car-mine when I responded: "You're blaming the victim for her victimization, and this is grossly immoral!"

As dinner was now certainly a thing of the past, the terse retort came back to me: "According to you and your beliefs this is immoral, but according to me and my beliefs this is perfectly moral." The evening was done and all that remained was for one of my dinner partner's past lives to pick up the tab.

Our dinner conversation brought us to the crux of the matter regarding living well: Is there truly a way to determine what the right and good way of life is? Is there a way that is not only good and right for me, but also for you? Everyone? To answer these questions we must get back on the road again with John Henry.

John Henry heard that the Chesapeake and Ohio Railroad is building a line through West Virginia. He arrives at the railroad only to find that work had stopped before a large mountain. A tunnel was going to have to be built, and quite a commotion was being stirred by the arrival of a new machine, a steam drill. No need for human efforts, let technology lead the way. But John Henry would have none of that. Knowing that convenience is a poor reason for living, he offers up a challenge. Steam drill on one side of the mountain and John Henry on the other side. Whoever gets further into the mountain when they meet, wins. The contest is agreed to, and John Henry is about to meet the challenge of his life.

The contest begins, each contestant digs into the mountain, and something unusual happens on John Henry's side. A rainbow that appeared whenever John Henry started flashing his hammers, left his shoulders and wrapped itself around the mountain for all to see. Now here, as John Henry burrows deep into the earth, is where we come to the deepest issue of living well: The goodness of John Henry's character, symbolized by the rainbow, is something that can be seen and judged by all those watching the contest. It represents a standard by which John Henry's life can objectively be evaluated. In other words, the rainbow represents *a consensual standard of goodness and rightness in conduct and character by which everyone's thoughts and actions can be measured in order to truly determine what living well is.* The measure of John Henry the man is more than the man himself. Yet, can you truly have a universal standard of living well?

When you start talking about universal standards of living well a lot of folks get downright uncomfortable. Undiscriminating relativists say there are no absolute truths (I once asked one of my professors if that was absolutely true), and thus no universal standards. They view the moral and spiritual highways as having no signs and signals to regulate the traffic. Unfortunately, that emphasis on freedom of choice and expression leads to a lot of crash and burns down the road of life. Conversely, narrow-minded absolutists can so over-regulate the traffic flow down the highways and byways of life that individual expression is inhibited and choice becomes illusory. I liken these two extreme positions to two ships. The *SS (stupid and silly) Relative* is like a sailing ship without a rudder. Whichever way the currents of fads go and winds of public opinion (usually hot air) blow, that's where relativism takes you. The *H.M.S. (horribly myopic sticklers) Absolute* is like a ship with a rudder that is fixed and can't be moved. The ship goes in one direction, and its course cannot be changed no matter what arises in the changing conditions of the human sea. Neither ship offers any real hope to the shipwrecked adrift on the tides of time. What is needed is a ship with a good compass and map and a rudder that can be steered according to those guides.

But what does this talk of roads and ships have to do with John Henry's rainbow? When I see John Henry's rainbow I see more than just the seven spectral colors of red, orange, yellow, green, blue, indigo, and violet. I see a standard of living flexible enough to meet the changing conditions of time, culture, and personal experience, yet firm enough to provide strong guidance for all who seek to truly live well. More specifically, the colors of the rainbow symbolize to me the seven virtues from antiquity: the Cardinal Virtues of the great Greek philosopher Plato—courage, justice, wisdom, and temperance—and the theological virtues of the apostle Paul—faith, hope, and love. These virtues (the defining marks of moral and spiritual excellence) are the touchstone of time and the crossroads of culture when it comes to determining a life lived well. It is my hope and prayer that, as we explore this rainbow of virtue in the symbolism of color and imagery, God will use these virtues as a compass to draw us closer to Him. But why wait to live well?

I Shall Not Pass This Way Again

Through this toilsome world, alas!
Once and only once I pass;
If a kindness I may show,
If a good deed I may do
To a suffering fellow man,
Let me do it while I can.
No delay, for it is plain
I shall not pass this way again.

—Author unknown

Courage

The ability to face adversity, danger, and fear with endurance, purpose, and inner strength

be with you wherever you go. —Joshua 1:9

do not be discouraged, for the Lord your God will

Chapter 2

The Red Badge of Courage

But one of the soldiers pierced
His side with a spear,
and immediately blood and water came out.

—John 19:34

LIKE MANY YOUNG BOYS AROUND THE WORLD, MY BOYS LIKE TO PLAY WITH toy soldiers. So, when I offered to read them Stephen Crane's Civil War story, *The Red Badge of Courage*, they eagerly jumped at the chance to hear about an adventure that would fit in so well with the imaginary battles that were being fought on their bedroom carpets, dressers, and about anyplace else a toy soldier could be placed. As we began the story they wanted to know what this red badge was. I told them that if they listened carefully to the story they would find out. Their ears perked up as the great Civil War battle of Chancellorsville began to unfold before them. The excited smiles began to change to looks of concern and consternation, however, as they realized what the red badge was. My children understood, albeit at a superficial level, that unlike their toy soldiers, horrible things happen to real soldiers as the earth receives back the spilt blood of those caught up in the storms of war. My children still play with their toy soldiers, but I hope and pray as they grow they will learn two lessons about wars.

First, there is evil in this world, and war is sometimes unavoidable—ask those like my father who fought against Hitler and the Nazis. However, there is no glory in the slaughter of human life. How can we rejoice in the pain, the suffering, and the shedding of blood of our fellow humans?

Second, it is a mistake to ignore and demean the sacrifices of those people who gave their lives for something greater than their own lives. I feel a sense of shame and anger each Veterans Day as the "enlightened" intellectuals on college campuses ignore and thereby demean the contributions of those men and women who fought so that they can have their cushy jobs. How can we forget the pain, the suffering, and the shedding of blood of those whose often-heroic sacrifices were made for you and me? How can I forget the bravery of my father, who barely survived the sinking of his destroyer by kamikaze planes off the coast of Okinawa during World War II? I want my children to know that there is no glory in war, but there is glory in the noble efforts of those who dare to wear the red badge of courage, and in the deeds of those whose actions shine like beacons of light in humanity's darkest hours.

My children wondered what the red badge was. They learned that the red badge is a symbol of courage. As my boys learned of the red badge, I began to think of the many ways the color red speaks of courage: Red is a passionate color, a color of power, energy, and strong emotion. When you see people of great courage, you will see people of great inner strength, vigor, and feeling. Feelings and emotions play an especially important role in fortitude. Through great *passion*, brave people are impelled to acts and compelled to face fears that others would shrink away from. They go forward no matter what the opposition.

"Forward, the Light Brigade!"
Was there a man dismay'd?
Not tho' the soldier knew
Someone had blunder'd:
Theirs not to make reply,
Theirs not to reason why,
Theirs but to do and die:
Into the valley of Death
Rode the six hundred.

Cannon to the right of them,
Cannon to the left of them,
Cannon in front of them
Valley'd and thunder'd;
Storm'd at with shot and shell,
Boldly they rode and well,
Into the jaws of Death,
Into the mouth of Hell
Rode the six hundred
            —from "The Charge of the Light Brigade" by Alfred Tennyson

It is not that the courageous lack fear; it is, like the Light Brigade, that they face their fears and move straight through their fears. Courage is a virtue that enables the bearer to master his or her fears rather than being mastered by them.

The passion of courage also empowers people to *persist* in their efforts and, if they fail, to get back up and try again. The true test of courage is not initial success, but what you do when success seems so elusive, when nothing seems to work out well, when all seems to fail. Many can show flashes of courage, moments of heroism. Yet, many a courageous man or woman has lost the spirit of fortitude under the test of enduring opposition. The heart of the truly courageous—those to whom courage is a way of life, rather than an occasional happenstance—is unyielding in the face of adversity. No matter what, they, as depicted in Carl Sandburg's poem "Upstream," keep coming on:

The strong men keep coming on.
They go down shot, hanged, sick, broken.
They live on fighting, singing,
lucky as plungers.

The strong men—they keep coming on.
The strong mothers pulling them
from a dark sea, a great prairie,
a long mountain.

Call hallelujah, call amen,
call deep thanks.
The strong men keep coming on.

One of the certainties I've learned in life is that I will fail. I've had some notable crashes and I've been burned enough to think that my middle name should be "toast". But I've also learned with certainty that where there is failure, there is opportunity to learn of courage, to fan the inner fires of passion and say, "I will keep coming on!"

Red, of course, as emphasized in Stephen Crane's story, is the color of blood. To be courageous means you have to *risk your blood*—your life—instead of being concerned with preserving your comforts and pleasures. To the courageous there is something to risk everything for, something—or, perhaps more often, *someone*—to spill blood for. It is no coincidence that the word *courage* is derived from the Latin word *cor*, which means "heart". People have long recognized the connection between courage and the willingness to sacrifice the red blood coming from your heart by calling the courageous names such as "stout-hearted", "iron-hearted", "great-hearted", or "strong of heart". As a Christian I pray that the whole world would recognize the connection between the shedding of Jesus Christ's blood and God's great love for humanity. I can not fully comprehend the courage of a man willing to shed his blood on a cross in order to take on *all the sins of humanity* to bridge the gap between the human heart and the heart of God. If you want to know courage, consider the crucifixion of Jesus, the God who gave His blood for you and me.

Lionhearted Living

> The lion, which is mightiest among beasts and turns not back before any . . . (Prov. 30:30)

When I was a young child my mother and father would take me shopping with them each week at the A & P Supermarket. I especially enjoyed the time when the supermarket offered for sale the *Golden Book Encyclopedia*. Each week a new letter volume came out. I loved going through those books, and some stories about ancient Greek heroes really caught my eye. In fact, decades later I can still see in my mind's eye brave Achilles dragging Hector around the walls of Troy. My interest in Greek history was stimulated, and I read many books about Argonauts, Olympian exploits, and of course, the Trojan War. Of all the stories I read, none left a greater impression on me than the true story of a Spartan king named Leonidas—a man whose calling in life reflected what he was called.

For two days, Leonidas and his small band of soldiers had held at bay the mightiest army in the world, the Persian army of Xerxes.

In spite of being outnumbered by over one hundred to one, Greek tenacity had humbled a vastly superior force at a pass called Thermopylae, between the mountains and the sea. Courage in the face of insurmountable odds ruled the day, but the second night brought the darkness of treachery that would soon test the limits of that courage.

A Greek traitor, willing to sell his honor and countrymen for material gain, had come to the camp of Xerxes. For the right price, he offered a secret path around the Greek stronghold at Thermopylae. The Persians, he suggested, could travel through that pass, wipe out the small Greek contingent guarding it, and then surround the determined Greeks at Thermopylae.

Xerxes was delighted to seize an opportunity to destroy a Spartan-lead obstacle that was greatly upsetting his plans to conquer Greece. The treacherous plan was put into effect and was successful. Only a few Greeks were able to escape and warn Leonidas.

Leonidas was faced with a dilemma. He could quickly order a retreat to avoid being surrounded, yet the rest of the Greeks desperately needed time to prepare their defenses. To stay would buy more time for Greece, but at the price of certain death. Leonidas made his decision. He ordered all his troops except his royal guard of three hundred Spartans and a few allies to escape through the mountains to fight another day. He and his brave comrades would stay and fight to the last man.

And fight to the last breath is what they did, staving off the surrounding Persians for yet another day. The Persians won the battle, but the courage of the king of Sparta had paved the way for an eventual Greek triumph in the war.

Prophetically, the parents of Leonidas named him after the lion. At the battle of Thermopylae in 480 B.C., Leonidas demonstrated the extent to which the lionhearted will go to follow the call of courage. There is much to learn about courage by examining the deeds of the lion of the pass at Thermopylae.

Leonidas knew that he was vastly outnumbered, but he decided to make a stand in *spite* of the overwhelming opposition. Such is the calling of the courageous today. Virtue is not the way of the many, and when you stand for moral and spiritual excellence you must have the courage to face great opposition.

Somebody said that it couldn't be done,
But he with a chuckle replied

That "maybe it couldn't," but he would be one
Who wouldn't say so till he'd tried.
                    —from "It Couldn't Be Done" by Edgar A. Guest

Being virtuous is not like competing in a popularity contest. Just the opposite is true. The more you stand for what is right and good, the louder the jeers, the greater the mockeries, the more delight people will have in your failures. It takes courage to say the unpopular thing, to bear up against personal attacks, to look around and see many against you and few for you. But those with a lion in their hearts will "not turn back before any" . . . or many.

The original plans of Leonidas were circumvented by a treacherous deed, and he had to resort to a different strategy. No matter how much courage is called out of the heart there is no guarantee that the first attempts will succeed or that courage will always win the day. You will find in the truly courageous not a smattering of impulsive acts, but instead a pattern of thoughtfulness and purposefulness that yields a habit of courageousness. This pattern of thinking is *flexible*, able to meet the changing needs and fluctuating demands. Sometimes courage must go on the offensive, such as verbally condemning the evil of pornography. At other times, courage must be on the defensive, such as refusing the view the lewdness and immorality that is placed before you. Courage may be public, in confronting and attacking the evils of the day. Courage may be private, in struggling against the fears, prejudices, and temptations that no one else knows you face.

There's many a battle fought daily
The world knows nothing about.
There's many a brave soldier
Whose strength puts a legion to rout.
And he who fights sin single-handed
Is more of a hero, I say,
Than he who leads soldiers to battle
And conquers by arms in the fray.
                    —from "Our Heroes" by Phoebe Cary

Whatever the case may be, courage is a battle fought on many fronts, in many ways, and requires an intelligent commander to know how to best win the victory.

Leonidas knew that ultimate victory against the Persians would require an immediate sacrifice. He believed that it was his responsibility to make that sacrifice. The longer people act courageously, the farther their vision goes. They see more the long-term goal rather than the short-term gains. They realize that failure to act courageously today is more often than not going to lead to greater problems in the future. Courage today is the greatest means to demoting future ills and promoting tomorrow's blessings. Ella Wheeler Wilcox in a line from her poem "You Never Can Tell" said it well:

> You never can tell when you do an act
> Just what the result will be,
> But with every deed you are sowing a seed,
> Though the harvest you may not see.

Courage today best ensures a future where far greater courage is not needed.

Faintheartedness

> . . . they are fainthearted and wasting away; there is trouble and anxiety like on a storm-tossed sea which cannot rest. (Jer. 49:23)

Courage is most apparent when it stands in contrast to its opposites, particularly cowardice, weakness, and timidity. The word *coward* literally means "with the tail between the legs." When it comes to danger or adversity, the coward does not face it, but instead turns tail and avoids it. This only leads to more problems, as opportunities to learn and grow are lost. What is likely gained is a growth in the power of the threat. Indeed, much evil in human history has come about because cowards failed to confront it before it grew to full power. Would there have been a holocaust if certain European leaders had the guts to stop Hitler before it was too late? I have learned in life that there is only one way to conquer fear: face it. When I have failed to do so, my cowardice has led to greater heartache down the road.

Cowards fit in well with the crowds. Those who refuse to stand up for the just cause do not like to stand out from the crowd. Many years ago, when I was a university student, several of my classmates and I got together to discuss a problem in class, namely that we believed that the professor was shirking his responsibilities and we weren't learning as much as we should. We decided to talk to the professor during the next class. We presented our complaints to him, and then he asked one of the students—one who had been most vociferous in registering his complaints about the professor in our student meeting—what he thought. The student replied he thought the class was "a breath of fresh air." I nearly choked on his fresh-air statement. Could this be the same person who was highly critical of the professor when with a group of students? How the tone and content changed when he had an opportunity to flatter the professor! Cowards are very fickle in which way they wag the tail; first this way, then that way—whichever way is most convenient, easiest, and quickest to self-gain.

Inner strength is the resource of the lionhearted; inner *weakness* the drawback of the fainthearted. It takes strength to stand against the gravity of sins that pull people down. Those without inner strength will easily lie down before the vices of society, the whims of the newest fad, the voices of popularity. To be courageous you must have a determination to be so. If you cannot call up within yourself the needed resolve, steadfastness, and endurance, the ways of fortitude will be fleeting moments, never truly in your grasp. The good news is that an honest recognition of your weakness is the first step toward becoming courageous. Many who seem to be strong are actually weak, as their "strength" is really a facade of prideful self-centeredness. Genuine strength is found in the humility that comes from admitting your weaknesses. The apostle Paul wrote that ". . . when I am weak, then I am strong" (2 Cor. 12:10). By looking to God rather than to self for the ultimate source of strength, an eternal foundation is laid for a courage that will truly pass the test of time.

A third attribute of faintheartedness is *timidity*, where a person is mastered by her or his fears. I grew up as a shy individual and I continue to remain on the introverted side of life. My timidity inhibited me in relationships and limited my career aspirations. As a little boy I loved to learn, but when my mother would call me the "little professor," I'd recoil at the thought of standing up in front of people and talking. Thus, it was a very strange turn of events that happened to me my second year of doctoral studies. I was working as a faculty research assistant, doing something so boring—one of those "brain optional" tasks—that I went to my professor and asked him if there was anything else I could do. He suggested teaching one of his classes. I immediately accepted, such was the pain of my boredom. Then, while walking out of his office, it hit me: *Yikes! What did I just say?* To make matters worse, here I was with stage fright, going to have to talk to approximately two hundred students on a subject I knew little about—child psychology—in a room where I must stand in front of the students on a theater stage of all places!

The dreaded day of the first class came, I climbed to the stage—hoping those in the back rows couldn't hear my heart pounding—and began to talk. Within just a few minutes a still small voice whispered to me: "This is what you're going to do for the rest of your life." Decades later I still marvel that I stand up in front of people talking for a living, and I *love* every minute of it—especially when I talk about children! Courage has its price, but I've learned that a greater price is paid when you can't overcome your fears.

The cowardly, weak, and timid live in the small worlds that they enclose themselves in. The courageous live large, for courage knows no bounds. Rudyard Kipling, in his "Ballad of East and West," said it succinctly.

> But there is neither East nor West,
> Border, nor Breed, nor Birth,
> When two strong men stand face to face,
> though they come from the ends of the earth!

Courage . . .

1. ensures that *justice* is meted out at all times to all people;
2. enables the voice of *wisdom* to be heard no matter what the adversity;
3. strengthens the *temperate* to remain in control when others are losing control;
4. emboldens the *faithful* to take that leap of faith and to walk faithfully with God no matter what the persecution or mockery;
5. stimulates the dare of *hoping* and the perseverance of hoping despite trying circumstances;
6. prompts us to *love* no matter what the possible hurt and, despite that hurt, to love again

. . . the inner strength of the lionhearted.

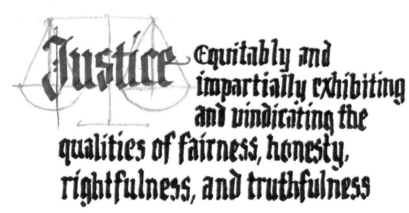

Justice Equitably and impartially exhibiting and vindicating the qualities of fairness, honesty, rightfulness, and truthfulness

Chapter 3

Is Justice Colorblind?

Righteousness and justice are the foundation of your throne; mercy, lovingkindness, and truth go before your face.

—Ps. 89:14

MY WIFE, KATHLEEN, WAS SITTING IN A LAW SCHOOL CLASS AT THE BEGINNING of the semester when the following question was posed by the professor: "An elderly lady has fallen into a lake and cannot save herself. You are her only means of rescue. This did not take place on your property and is not your fault. Do you have any legal obligation to save the lady?" The class overwhelmingly responded affirmatively and were immediately corrected by the professor who said that they were wrong: They had no legal obligation to save the lady. Several weeks later the same question was asked by the professor in class. This time the students overwhelmingly responded in the way they were taught: They had no legal obligation to help that woman. Kathleen, who did not go along with the new majority opinion, was shocked, not as much by the students' responses—legally speaking, this was the right answer—but by what was happening to the students. The law school education was splitting apart the practice of law from the moral and spiritual aspects of justice, discarding the latter in favor of the former. What type of people were these students of "justice" becoming in learning to separate their legal duties from that which is compassionate and right?

Kathleen did not finish her law school education, choosing instead to work in the field of psychology with the victims of injustice. She usually works with victims who have the greatest difficulty finding justice in our society: young children. Her work with abused and neglected children has led to a lot of involvement with the legal system. She has told me too many stories of dishonest lawyers, lazy attorneys, and people working in the supposed justice system who really don't care and are blinded by their prejudices, biases, and social agendas. Did these people sit in classes like my wife once did? Perhaps some of these people have crossed over the line of what's right so many times that the line has been erased. Maybe they are so burned out in their professions that they can no longer genuinely care about people or justice. I'm really not too concerned about the excuses. I am greatly concerned about the reasons why justice is so frequently perverted. I admire my wife because she uncompromisingly stands for what's right and compassionate for her clients. She will fight for justice where most others will give up. I am honored to be married to such a virtuous woman. But I am saddened and angered that people like my wife are, bluntly, a minority in the justice system. What can the righteous do if the foundations of justice are destroyed? (See Ps. 11:3)

The problem with the justice system is that a relativistic philosophy has obscured the vision of those who work in that system. They can't clearly see the foundations of justice. What are those foundations? I see a threefold foundation in the color I have chosen for justice: orange. If you mix red and yellow paint together, you get orange paint. If you want to get justice, you'll have to add in those two colors that stand for three crucial components of justice.

The first color to add into "justice paint" is yellow—the color of *wisdom*. Justice must be based on wise principles, decisions must be wisely rendered, and consequences must be derived in wisdom. Just men and women will seek out the facts, determine the pertinence of those facts, insightfully and skillfully use those facts in resolving the matter at hand, and with great forethought, understand the implications for future matters of justice. They will be blind to biases, bribes, and the misleading influences of eloquent words, but keensighted in regard to fairness and the pursuit of truth. Without wisdom, justice would only be an occasional happenstance.

The second ingredient of justice is red—the color of courage and passion. Courage is necessary because just people will often have to stand against the fickle tides of public outrage and adulation. Justice rarely travels with the crowd. When is the last time you heard about a mob setting out to do good? When people get caught up in a crowd, they usually lose their sense of individual responsibility and fling away whatever moral and spiritual principals they have. Moses wrote about this in the Book of Exodus (23:2): "You shall not follow a crowd to do evil; nor shall you bear witness at a trial so as to side with a multitude to pervert justice." I praise my wife for refusing to go along with the crowd of law school students who agreed that they had no legal obligation to help the imperiled woman. She continues to refuse to go along with those who would pervert justice for her clients. I praise her courage for not going along with the unjust, maddening crowd.

Hand-in-hand with the courage to stand for justice is the passion to *fight for right*. The descent from justice is a slippery slope paved in lazy indifference and greased by cowardly apathy. Justice is not the natural course of a world driven by self-pleasure and motivated by survival of the fittest. No, justice is more concerned with restraining pleasures for the common good and helping the least fit to survive. Justice is always going to be a fight against the dark places of the human soul. It will always take people with a burning desire to help the unfortunate, to right the wrong, to defeat the evil, if justice is to be brought about. Great justice will only occur if there are passionate people of great heart.

> Give us men!
> Men who, when the tempest gathers,
> Grasp the standard of their fathers
> In the thickest fight;
> Men who strike for home and altar,
> (Let the coward cringe and falter),
> God defend the right!
> True as truth the lorn and lonely,
> Tender, as the brave are only;
> Men who tread where saints have trod,
> Men for Country, Home—and God:
> Give us Men! I say again—again—
> Give us Men!
> —from "Give Us Men!" by Josiah Gilbert Holland

The yellow of wise principals and actions and the red of courage and passion are necessary for justice. But I see another essential ingredient for justice in a tranquil, toned-down version of red: the pink voice of *compassion, mercy, and undeserved lovingkindness*. The 89th psalm paints a picture of a God who is, on one hand, absolutely just—"righteousness, justice, truth"—and on the other hand, absolutely loving—"mercy and lovingkindness." In other words, God is a judge incorruptible when it comes to what is just, and inescapable when it comes to forgiving those breeches of justice. Many people can't envision a God who exhibits both of those qualities. They'll say things like, "How can a loving God send people to hell?" People find it easy to accept the loving God and convenient to reject the just God. Those two aspects seem impossible to reconcile for most people.

Even theologians, priests, and ministers of God seem to avoid that apparent paradox by either avoiding the topic of God's justice (especially hell) or stripping God of His cloak of justice: "A loving God would not condemn to hell a person for . . ." A God who lets us be comfortable with however we choose to live is the only God many people are comfortable with. However, that's a nonbiblical idol.

Being absolutely just and absolutely merciful are not contradictory. In fact, they require one another. How can you be merciful unless there is first some standard of justice that has been violated? In other words, to forgive others of their wrongs requires that there first be something that is identified as wrong. To be merciful requires a reason why that mercy is indeed merciful. Conversely, justice needs mercy. Justice without mercy is a brother to oppression and a sister to enslavement. Imagine that God was just and not merciful. Consider that every single person has at some time violated His standard of justice (see Rom. 3:23) and therefore is deserving of eternal condemnation (see Rom. 6:23). What would be God's point in creating a standard that prevents every one of his created beings from being able to enjoy eternal life with their Creator? What kind of father would I be if I only accepted my children if they perfectly attained an impossible standard? A brute without a soul, that's what I would be. But because I love my children *before* they even know what standards of conduct they are expected to follow (don't lie, cheat, steal, etc.), I will love them and be able to forgive them before there is something to forgive.

Likewise, God, *before* a human being ever violated His standard of justice, loved us and was able to forgive us of any breach of His law. Because God is wholly merciful, He can be wholly just. Because there is no doubt about God's justice, there can be no doubt that He is merciful. The 85th psalm illustrates that well: "Mercy, lovingkindness, and truth have met together; righteousness and peace have kissed each other."

A Balancing Act

> A just balance and scales are the Lord's. . . . (Prov. 16:11)

Most people are familiar with the expression "I see the handwriting on the wall." This is commonly understood to mean that you have a good idea of what is about to happen. Historically, the expression is derived from the fifth chapter of the Book of Daniel. Here a story is told of the wicked king of Babylon, Belshazzar, who at a party to celebrate the greatness of his pride, was dumbfounded along with his guests when a hand suddenly appeared and wrote a few words on the wall. Nobody could figure out what the words meant, and as a last resort, a relic from a past age was brought in—Daniel—and asked to decipher the message. Fittingly, Daniel refused the king's offer of rewards and proceeded to courageously translate a message of doom to Belshazzar: "mene [numbered], tekal [weighed], parsin [divided]." Daniel then boldly expounded upon those words by telling Belshazzar that they meant his rule was weighed in the balance, found to be unjust, and his days were numbered—kingship terminated. In fact, the next day Belshazzar was dead and there were new rulers of the shattered Babylonian empire.

I love the imagery of the words on the wall. It's as if God has placed Belshazzar's wickedness on one side of the scales and the standard of goodness on the other. The weight of his wickedness tipped the scales so much to one side that it had to be removed. And so went Belshazzar. And so go we all. I believe "mene, tekel, parsin" has relevance to us all. Our days—our lifespan—are numbered before God; He is weighing us in the scales of justice, and without the intervention of the judge Himself, we will be divided from God for eternity. What does God weigh in the scales of justice?

An obvious answer to the aforementioned question would be that God puts all our good deeds and thoughts on one side of the scales and all our bad acts and imaginations on the other. I believe that God does this (see Rev. 20:12); but justice is more than just a matter of weighing personal wrongs and rights. Justice must be understood at the *individual and the corporate* levels. In other words, justice will involve a balancing act between my rights and others' rights, my needs and others' needs, what's good for me and what's good for society. Just people will work for what is right, realize that they are not always right, recognize the rights of others, and contribute to the welfare of others even if things aren't quite the way they think they should be. Just societies are arranged for the common good and ensure that fairness, impartiality, and honesty regulate all societal transactions. People must be willing to be just, fair, and honest with others if a just society is to be maintained. When people become more concerned with what others contribute than with what they contribute, a ripple of selfish injustice grows in intensity and magnitude and society must use sterner and eventually unjust means to gain those needed contributions.

On the other hand, societies must be willing to recognize the rights of the individual and the innate worthiness of being a human being, or freedoms will be trampled and people will not be taught that they are free to choose to be and do that which is good and right. Justice for all requires a mutual contract between the individual and society. That's why I believe that God not only judges individuals, but also nations. Furthermore, the judgments are inseparable when God is weighing the evidence. Christians cannot afford to excuse themselves from the policies of their nations. Look what the Nazis were able to achieve in Germany when that largely happened in the 1930s.

Also, inseparable in God's scales are the concrete reality of a person's life and the *abstract ideals* of the standard of justice. People may offer to God what they consider to be the good and bad deeds of their lives, but God will not weigh just their goodness against their badness. Instead, God weighs the good and the bad against *His* standard. I had a conversation with a man who basically said that God judges people based on their good versus bad deeds, not on whether or not they believe in Jesus Christ. He said that he couldn't believe that God would send good people to hell. A lot of folks agree with that man. From a Christian point of view there are at least two problems with that thinking. First is the idea that if you have enough good deeds, you'll tip the scales and get God's favor. The problem is that as long as there is *one* sin, the scales cannot be tilted enough to earn God's favor (again, see Rom. 6:23). Second, is the idea that you can adequately compare good deeds against bad deeds. The problem with this is that it assumes God measures a person only against oneself. Imagine going before a judge because of a speeding ticket and telling her that you shouldn't be fined because you normally go much faster than what you were ticketed for. She'd say—I hope—that it is not a matter of what you personally do better or worse, it's a matter of violating a standard. The good and bad deeds of a person's life are not on opposite sides of the scale; they are opposite God's standard. And, by the way, I believe God's standard requires Jesus Christ (see John 3:1–21).

I am not saying that what we think and do doesn't matter. Certainly "just desserts"—as people give, so should they receive—is a cornerstone of justice. Just as certain, our works have eternal consequences in regard to heaven (see 1 Cor. 3:15) and hell (see Matthew 11:21–24). God wants us to *know* the beauty of His standard of justice and to *live* in the light of this beauty.

> Beautiful faces are those that wear—
> It matters little if dark or fair—
> Whole-souled honesty printed there.
>
> Beautiful eyes are those that show,
> Like crystal panes where hearthfires glow,
> Beautiful thoughts that burn below.
>
> Beautiful lips are those whose words
> Leap from the heart like songs of birds,
> Yet whose utterance prudence girds.
>
> Beautiful hands are those that do
> Work that is honest and brave and true,
> Moment by moment the long day through.
>
> Beautiful feet are those that go
> On kindly ministries to and fro,
> Down lowliest ways, if God wills it so.
>
> Beautiful shoulders are those that bear
> Ceaseless burdens of homely care
> With patient grace and daily prayer.
>
> Beautiful lives are those that bless
> Silent rivers of happiness,
> Whose hidden fountains but few may guess.
> —from "Beautiful Things" by Ellen P. Allerton

A False Balance

> A false balance and unrighteous dealings are extremely offensive and shamefully sinful to the Lord, but a just weight is His delight. (Prov. 11:1)

Did you know the word *lawyer* and the word *lie* are derived from the same Indo-European root word, *legh?* Do you find this surprising? Don't, after all, *lawyer* and *lie* have a lot in common? Isn't it well known that *lawyer* refers to a profession and *lie* refers to a lawyer's practice? Well, I too see a lot in common with those two words, but I've misled you as to the basis for their commonality.

You see, *law* and *lie* do share a common origin, but it's not the *lie* that probably first came to your mind—the one that means "what a liar does." That word has a different origin than *law*. The *lie* that shares a common origin with *law* is the word that means "to lay down." Originally, *law* meant something that was "laid down" for all to follow and be judged by. Did the connotation of *liar* first come to your mind when you read about *lawyer* and *lie*? Why is it that a profession that is so intimately involved with the justice system is so easily linked with a word that means a departure from the truth and what is right? I need to be careful here because there are many honest, upright lawyers, some of whom I count among my friends. I have found, however, that there are too many lawyers for whom lying is second nature. What a great irony to find so many unjust individuals using and exploiting the justice system. What a stench in the nostrils of those who work for justice to see facts twisted and truth perverted in the name of "legal representation," with little or no thought given to what is right and best for society. Perhaps lawyers have just gotten a bad rap. Wouldn't almost anybody in their shoes do the same sort of things? But is that a good excuse? Morally and spiritually, should we have just anybody working in the justice system? No, I believe the higher the calling, the greater the responsibility to live up to that calling. If you represent justice, then you should be *more* honest, trustworthy, fair, and *blind* to bribes, agendas, and self-gain.

One of the great problems in bringing about justice is how to restore justice after it has been breached. For example, in the United States there has been a long history of oppression against people of African origin. While the twentieth century witnessed great strides in overcoming that injustice, it would be a misstatement to say that by the end of the twentieth century the effects of that oppression had been eradicated. So, what to do about it? You have those that say that playing field is now level and nothing else needs to be done. On the other hand, you have those who would "level" the playing field by putting people of different racial and ethnic origins at a disadvantage in various social programs. Do you ignore injustice or use more injustice to supposedly correct past injustice? Greatly tilting the scales of justice either way would only lead to further injustice. Any way you cut it, because people are concerned with *self-gain*, because people publicly *posture* themselves to look like "good people," because people are *more* concerned about "my rights" than "your rights," the scales of justice are extremely difficult to balance. Furthermore, it would be impossible to balance the scales as long as justice is only looked at in the short-term, rather than the long-term—past and future. Justice must be blind to self-centered aims, but keensighted in regard to effecting a true, enduring justice. Few people, I am sad to say, can meet those two qualifications.

Where there are wise, courageous, truthful, and selfless people, there is hope that justice will rule the land. But, if there is not some understanding of an ultimate standard upon which justice is based, the reality of justice will be about as firm as a jellyfish in a bowl of Jell-O. Justice needs something solid to be founded on; it needs a backbone. Justice needs people who will seek out the ideals of what is right and good. People *lacking* in ideals find it easy to compromise justice and commit *venal* acts—selling themselves out for self-gain. I once had a discussion with an aspiring actor. He told me that an accomplished actor gave him the following advice: "If you want to make it in this business, you have to sell out." In other words, muzzle your morals, ditch your dignity, and sacrifice your scruples. I told that young man that if you take that actor's advice, you will be "selling your soul to the devil," and the devil is not good at giving back what he takes. I'm pleased to say that the young man did not sell out. He's not an actor, but he still has his soul.

Soul food—that's what the evil of injustice feeds on. An expensive meal. What's your price? I asked this to students in my class one time, and I was surprised by how many students reported they would do almost anything for enough money. Kathleen once taught an Introductory Psychology class, and she told me that nearly a quarter of the students reported that they'd kill someone for a million dollars if they knew they wouldn't get caught and the victim was a real slime ball! Without a moral and spiritual backbone—the ideals of justice—injustice can readily take any shape.

God, give us men and women who won't sell out their principals and will not corrupt Your ideals.

> God, give us men. A time like this demands
> Strong minds, great hearts, true faith and ready hands;
> Men whom the lust of office does not kill;
> Men whom the spoils of office cannot buy;
> Men who possess opinions and a will;
> Men who have honor; men who will not lie;
> Men who can stand before a demagogue
> And damn his treacherous flatteries without winking!
> Tall men, sun-crowned, who live above the fog
> In public duty and in private thinking;
> For while the rabble, with their thumb-worn creeds,
> Their large professions and their little deeds,
> Mingle in selfish strife, lo! Freedom weeps,
> Wrong rules the land and waiting Justice sleeps.
> —from "God, Give Us Men!" by Josiah Gilbert Holland

Yes, Lord. Give us women and men like that!

Justice . . .

1. serves as the conscience of *courage,* giving courage direction and purpose;
2. demands that the fruits of *wisdom* are properly and appropriately discovered and shared with others;
3. stands against the societal evils—greed, lust, and perverted desires—of intemperance, yet instills in the *temperate* a consideration and compassion for those wounded by intemperance;
4. gives people a reason to trust, to have *faith* in others and God;
5. sows seeds of trust and therefore optimism, providing a fertile soil for the sprouting of *hope;*
6. works for what is best for others, the action of *loving;*

. . . balancing the scales of God's ideals with passion and wisdom.

it cost all you have, get understanding. —— Proverbs 4:6——7

Though therefore get wisdom. Wisdom is supreme; over you. Wisdom is supreme; therefore get wisdom. Though

WISDOM

The ability to use knowledge
perceptively, discreetly, and
skillfully in evaluating,
deciding upon, and following
the soundest course of action

Chapter 4

Yellow Gold

Therefore I counsel you to purchase from Me gold refined and tested by fire, that you may be truly wealthy. . . .

—Rev. 3:18

GOLD IS A PRECIOUS YELLOW METAL THAT HAS BEEN OF GREAT VALUE SINCE THE earliest days of the human race. People have done almost anything to get it. Men and women have sold their homes and moved great distances in hopes of finding it. Paupers, princes and princesses, and all sorts of people in between have coveted it. Individuals have murdered to steal it; nations have declared war because of it. Lovers wear it proudly on their fingers; proud royals of ancient days dressed their tombs in it. No other metal has held such an esteemed place in human history. No other substance has been compared more to wisdom. What is it about gold that sparks such ready comparisons to wisdom?

Gold has many fine qualities, but there are four important attributes that I believe speak of the richness of wisdom. The first of these attributes is that gold is very *attractive* in its brightness and color. In other words, it is desirable to behold. Have you ever met a truly wise person? Truly bright people exude an attractive quality that is desirable to behold. I have met some very wise individuals in my life, and their words have left lasting impressions on me. Wise words that have given me insight into my life, the way of the world, and the way of the Spirit have been precious to me. Imagine the joy and excitement of a prospector tediously panning for gold in a streambed when suddenly his or her eye is caught by the shining brilliance of a gold nugget! How much more precious the nuggets of wisdom found in the streams of human words. I once found such gold in the midst of those streams. When I was eleven years old I was given a King James Bible. I rarely looked at it and never bothered to read it. Eleven years later, when I became a Christian, I suddenly discovered that within the dusty pages of that book was a gold mine of wisdom—eternal truths. There was a psalm (19:7–11) that I learned to sing in the first Bible study I attended that still has a special meaning to me in this regard:

> The law of the Lord is perfect, converting the soul:
> the testimony of the Lord is sure, making wise the simple.
> The statutes of the Lord are right, rejoicing the heart:
> the commandment of the Lord is pure, enlightening the eyes.
> The fear of the Lord is clean, enduring forever:
> the judgments of the Lord are true, and righteous altogether.
>
> [Chorus]
> More to be desired are they than gold,
> yea, than much fine gold:
> sweeter also than honey and the honeycomb.
>
> Moreover by them is thy servant warned:
> and in keeping of them,
> there is great reward.

Those who have a heart for wisdom will desire wisdom more than any material good. Their lives will reflect the brilliance of that which they gaze upon. Maybe that's why the face of Moses glowed after being with God on Mount Sinai. (See Exod. 34)

A second important attribute of gold is that it is the most malleable and ductile of all metals. In other words, it is easily worked with, is readily shaped in a diversity of forms, and is not brittle. In fact, gold is so pliant that an ounce of it can be beaten out into thin sheets of gold leaf to the size of nearly two hundred square feet.

Wisdom has great *coverage* too. Have you ever been awestruck by the beauty of a masterful painting? Has great music ever sent goosebumps up your arms? Has a great speech ever left you speechless? Have the words of the Spirit of the living God ever taken your breath away? Wisdom can reach into the human soul in a variety of ways and effect the same result: an unbroken link with eternity. How good it feels to speak the fitting word: "like apples of gold in settings of silver" (Prov. 25:11). How instructive it is to have the fitting word spoken to you: "like . . . an ornament of fine gold is a wise reprover to an ear that listens and obeys" (Prov. 25:12). Wherever and however wisdom is found, it has the power to shape a human life into the image of God.

The third noteworthy attribute of gold is that it does not tarnish or corrode. It is virtually indestructible. When I read Plato, Aristotle, or the words of other great thinkers of antiquity, I find truths that are as relevant today as they were thousands of years ago. I see something even greater in the words of Moses, the prophets, the apostles, and of course, Jesus Christ. Wisdom can stretch through all eternity, untarnished by time, not destroyed by the ages. In fact, the test of wisdom is how long it can stand the *test of time*. Wisdom is not, however, only to be found in the past. There are those who are wedded to the wisdom of the past who divorce themselves from the wisdom of the present and future. There are Christians who hold on to the fact that "God has spoken" but refuse to reach out their hands to the "God who is speaking." Wise people cherish the wisdom of the past and open their eyes to the wisdom of the present age. Wisdom of any age is a friend to those who are wise of heart.

> Make new friends, but keep the old;
> Those are silver, these are gold.
> New-made friendships, like new wine,
> Age will mellow and refine.
> Friendships that have stood the test—
> Time and change—are surely best;
> Brow may wrinkle, hair grow gray,
> Friendship never knows decay.
> For 'mid old friends, tried and true,
> Once more we our youth renew.
> But old friends, alas! may die,
> New friends must their place supply.

Cherish friendship in your breast—
New is good, but old is best;
Make new friends, but keep the old;
Those are silver, these are gold.
　　　　—from "New Friends and Old Friends" by Joseph Parry

The final attribute of gold that makes me think of wisdom is its *origin*. It is believed that gold has been carried up from great depths in the earth. Furthermore, it is usually found in nature in a relatively pure form. When I think of "the depths" and purity, I think of Romans 11:33: "Oh, the depths of the riches and wisdom and knowledge of God! . . ." I believe that ultimately all wisdom is from God and that truly wise people will be led to God in their thirst for knowledge. Proverbs 9:10 says, "The reverent and worshipful fear of the Lord is the beginning of Wisdom, and the knowledge of the Holy One is insight and understanding." God founded the earth and heavens by His wisdom (see Prov. 3:19), and in the marvelous complexity of design of this planet and the universe, wise people will find God. Those on the cutting edge of scientific discoveries often cut God out of the process, and in their myopic thoughts cannot see the work of God. However, when great intelligence is matched by great humility and open-mindedness, God can be seen. The deepest wisdom is inseparable from the pure and holy God.

A Stroke of Wisdom

The king said, One says, This is my son that is alive and yours is the dead one. The other woman says, No! But your son is the dead one and mine is the living one.

And the king said, Bring me a sword. And they brought a sword to the king.

And the king said, Divide the living child in two and give half to the one and half to the other.

Then the mother of the living child said to the king, for she yearned over her son, O my lord, give her the living baby, and by no means slay him. But the other said, Let him not be mine or yours, but divide him.

Then the king said, Give her [who pleads for his life] the living baby, and by no means slay him. She is the child's mother.

And all Israel heard of the judgment which the king had made, and they stood in awe of him, for they saw the wisdom of God was in him to do justice. (1 Kings 3:23–28)

It is fitting that the sword should play a prominent role in this prototypical story of Solomon's wisdom. The sword symbolizes the ability to cut through the dross of useless and misleading information, so as to discover the precious gold of truth. In the above story, Solomon is presented with a case in which the truth is hard to determine. I find it enlightening in how he went about discovering the truth. In the verses preceding those presented, two women are brought before Solomon and present their cases to him. Importantly, no words of Solomon are recorded. He sits on his throne and listens to the claims of both parties. I have found that wise people do a lot more *listening* than talking. They follow the sage advice "Since we have two ears and one mouth, we should listen twice as much as we speak."

Furthermore, he listens to *both sides* of the story before speaking. Wisdom is a double-edged sword that is made to cut in more than one direction. Much foolishness occurs when we listen to only one side of the story. When there are competing claims to the truth, it is wise to listen to all the claims before making a decision. After listening, Solomon speaks. But, the words he speaks are not his final decision. Instead, he sets up a test to determine who the real mother is. He uses a sword to metaphorically pierce the heart of the true mother, whom he knows could not bear to witness the death of her child. Before making a decision, the wisest course is to *evaluate* and *test* what you have been told or observed. Finally, at the right time, Solomon renders a decision. He could have set up more tests. He could have placed the child in some kind of Israelite foster home for months, perhaps years, until he did enough evaluation that he was absolutely sure, beyond a shadow of a doubt, that he was correct in his judgment. Wisdom, however, often requires a risk. There are times when we have to make decisions on the basis of what we know, even though our knowledge is limited and incomplete. My beautiful wife accepted my proposal for marriage even though there was much she didn't know about me. Being wise does not require being perfect in your knowledge; it requires *acting* upon what you know. Solomon was considered wise not just because of what he knew, but because of what he did with that knowledge.

That brings us to the salient fact about wisdom: *It's not how much you know, but how much you do with what you know.* I remember listening to the advice of a brilliant doctoral student my first year of doctoral studies. The student had been in the program for a few years, and I was impressed by his intellectual acumen. When I received my doctorate in that program five years later, he was still working on finishing his doctoral studies. I was then impressed by his inability to do something constructive with his great IQ. I think he misunderstood the advice given in the following poem:

> If a task is once begun
> Never leave it till it's done
> Be the labor great or small,
> Do it well or not at all.
> —from "Always Finish," author unknown

I've had many students in my classes who have followed that man's lead. High IQs and low grades—what a waste! Give me average students with an above-average desire to complete what they finish and to do what they do well, rather than the other way around, any day of the week! There's wisdom in those who wield the sword they've been given. There's foolishness in those given fine swords and who won't put them to use. I'd rather go to battle in the small ranks of the wise than with a large company of fools. Wisdom is knowledge in *action*; foolishness is knowledge *inaction*.

Like a fencer who must practice long hours to be successful in a duel, so too the success of putting knowledge into action is greatly affected by experience. That's why you typically find wisdom residing more in older rather than younger people. The United States of America was most fortunate to have the experience of a very wise, older man, George Washington, during the earliest years of the nation. One of his wisest acts involved what he did with his sword in 1783 . . . The Revolutionary War was won. As commander-in-chief of American forces, George Washington was the most powerful man on the continent. He could have easily installed himself as a dictator. Instead, he surrendered his sword to the Continental Congress, symbolically submitting himself and the military under the desires of the people of the land. The wisdom of his action and the consequences it has had on the strength of the American nation have over two hundred years of confirming witness. I have read that many European leaders were shocked that a man who wielded such power would give up that power. But knowledge tempered in experience led Washington to do something many, perhaps most, people in his position would not have done. Washington saw an opportunity to establish a strong democracy that others did not see. That's the eye of the wise person: seeing and taking advantage of opportunities that are easily overlooked by lesser folks.

> This I beheld, or dreamed it in a dream:
> There spread a cloud of dust along a plain;
> And underneath the cloud, or in it, raged
> A furious battle, and men yelled, and swords
> Shocked upon swords and shields. A prince's banner
> Wavered, then staggered backward, hemmed by foes.
> A craven hung along the battle's edge
> And thought, "Had I a sword of keener steel—
> That blue blade that the king's son bears—but this
> Blunt thing—!" He snapt and flung it from his hand,
> And, lowering, crept away and left the field.
> Then came the king's son, wounded, sore bested,
> And weaponless, and saw the broken sword,
> Hilt-buried in the dry and trodden sand,
> And ran and snatched it, and with battle-shout
> Lifted afresh, he hewed his enemy down,
> And saved a great cause that heroic day.
> —from "Opportunity" by Edward Rowland Sill

All Christians have a wonderful sword of wisdom at their disposal. It's called "the sword that the Spirit wields, which is the Word of God" (Eph. 6:17). Jesus Christ used it effectively while dueling with Satan in the wilderness, depending upon scriptures to fend off the enemy (see Matt. 4:1–11). The Book of Revelation says that Jesus will completely vanquish that foe at the end of this age with the same weapon (see Rev. 1:16; 19:21).

It is a sword that is easily misused by those whose hearts do not truly follow the King of Kings. But to the true of heart, great success has been achieved. Great failures have been had, however, by those who have depended on their own abilities rather than waiting to be patiently taught by their Master. And, what stupidity to go into battle without it! Christians, cherish your swords, for many are those who would break them and thereby separate you from the only wise God.

Worshiping the Golden Image

> Then the herald cried aloud, O peoples, nations, and languages,
> That when you hear the sound of the horn, pipe, lyre, trigon, harp,
> dulcimer and bagpipe, and every kind of music, you are to fall

down and the worship the golden image that King Nebuchadnezzar has set up. (Dan. 3:4–5)

Nebuchadnezzar, king of ancient Babylon, was a man of enor-
mous accomplishment, with one great weakness: his *pride*. Prideful people are not happy unless other people can recognize and
applaud their "greatness." I wonder if that's why Nebuchadnezzar
set up the golden image. With great fanfare, others were to worship the golden image—perhaps the symbol of Nebuchadnezzar's
"wisdom"—that was set up. Nebuchadnezzar's weakness is the
same with all people of great accomplishment who lose sight of
their humble place in this universe.

I find this to be particularly true among learned men and women.
Now, there is satisfaction in doing something well, and it's nice to
be recognized by others for your accomplishments. However, that
often turns into a temptation when taken too far. I've often wondered why so many college campuses are poisoned by professors
who are constantly putting their colleagues down and can't stop
bickering with the administration. I've had fellow professors come
to me and tell me what other colleagues are saying about me behind my back. I usually have the same thing to say, "Tell so-and-so
that if s/he wants to discuss something with me, just come to my
office and we can talk face to face." Of course, they never come. I
have come to the conclusion that the toxic atmosphere found on
many college campuses comes from the egotistical arrogance of
people who profess to be wise in their own eyes. Heaven forbid
that you should not worship with great fanfare the monuments—
publications, speeches, etc.—of their greatness. A fiery furnace of
criticism awaits to take you down. People have long set up golden
images to celebrate their own supposed wisdom (see Exod. 32:2; 1
Kings 12:28). True wisdom, however, is found in the humility spoken of in 1 Peter 5:6: "Therefore humble yourselves under the mighty
hand of God, that in due time He may exalt you."

If you are familiar with the story of the golden image, then you
are probably familiar with the miraculous survival of Shadrach,
Meshach, and Abednego in the fiery furnace. How did they end up
in such a predicament? Daniel 3:8 explains how: "Therefore at that
time certain men of Chaldean descent came near and brought accu-
sations against the Jews." Shadrach, Meshach, and Abednego were
known for their wisdom (see Dan. 1:20), and that gained them en-
emies. In my mind's eye, I have seen those Chaldean betrayers and

I know them by their names. There are four of them, each an enemy of wisdom.

Envy has always been a sworn enemy of wisdom. She is always worried that somebody might have something more than she does. She can't stand the acclaim that others get for being wise. The good that wise people can do for others pales in comparison to how bad she feels that it is not her getting praised. You will find her finding fault with others. Her motto is "It's easier to criticize rather than create."

Mockery comes from a long line of scoffers. Wisdom has always been threatening to him. At one time he called himself Ishmael and made fun of Isaac. Later, he dressed up as a soldier and made fun of Jesus Christ. After he helped kill Jesus, he took the robes of a philosopher and made good sport of Paul at the Areopagus. He still loves to hang around with the "learned crowd." You will find him the life of the party, always jesting at the expense of others. His motto is "Let's jest have fun."

Craftiness is the most difficult one of the four to find. She is a master of disguise. She is skilled at taking knowledge that could be used in the service of others and turning into a means for self-serving aims. A sly creature, she's hard to spot because she doesn't want anybody to get a good look at her face. Nobody knows what her true motto is.

Nobody, however, has problems spotting *foolishness;* he's always drawing attention to himself. Known for his excessive wordiness (see Prov. 17:28), he's mastered the art of saying a whole lot about very little. He's often found in the company of politicians. His motto, unfortunately, is much too long to print here.   He, like his three companions, will never know the source of wisdom.

> All things bright and beautiful,
> All creatures great and small,
> All things wise and wonderful,
> The Lord God made them all.
> —from "All Things Bright and Beautiful" by Mrs. Alexander

Wisdom . . .

1. functions as the compass of *courage*, prudently guiding the actions of the courageous;

2. instructs the just how to implement *justice* and illuminates the difference between right and wrong, true and false;
3. steers the *temperate* between the excesses of over-control and under-control to the freedom of self-control;
4. informs you who you can put your *faith* in;
5. provides a rational basis for genuine *hope*;
6. teaches *lovers* how to know and understand each other and how to best do what is best for others;

. . . knowing what to do with the knowing.

Temperance

Self-control that leads to moderation and restraint in the pursuit and expression of pleasures and passions

Chapter 5

Greener Pastures

He makes me lie down in green pastures,
He leads me beside quiet waters,
He restores my soul.
He guides me in paths of righteousness
for His name's sake. (Ps. 23:2–3)

The world is too much with us; late and soon,
Getting and spending, we lay waste our powers:
Little we see in Nature that is ours;
We have given our hearts away, a sordid boon!
    —from "The World Is Too Much with Us" by William Wordsworth

PEACE OF MIND—THE MORE WE HAVE, THE LESS WE HAVE. WE GET THE HIGH-paying jobs, the big homes, expensive cars, and all the adult toys of a prosperous society. We strive to "make it" in material society and we lose something. The higher we climb the ladder of success, the farther away the simple tranquillity of a mind at peace seems to be. The more we surround ourselves with the technological trappings of a fast-paced society, the less likely we take time to slow down and seek the green pastures. What a shame. For in those green pastures are the quiet waters of the soul, which lead us in the paths of God. In those green pastures we find a virtue called temperance—forgotten in a world that beckons us to "have it all—now!", but never forsaken by those who wish to have it all . . . *eternally*, the ultimate peace of mind.

I've done some informal surveys in several of my college classes, asking my students to report which of the seven virtues they have greatest difficulty living out. Temperance, consistently, is the most frequent choice. No wonder. In a society driven by "Buy now, pay later," in a culture where fun and drugs—particularly alcohol—are seen to be inseparable, in a media-shaped world where sex out of marriage is glorified (How often is sexuality portrayed among married couples in the movies?), it is not surprising that college students should have a hard time finding temperance in their lives. They see so little of it in the world around them. My guess is that, should I do similar surveys among different, noncollege populations, I would find similar results. Things, drugs, sex—the world's tripartite way to satisfaction. But what is gained in the world is lost before the triune God. What is lost before God is the virtue of temperance and the lasting strength of the "green peace" of mind it confers upon its bearers. What is this temperance so important in the sight of God, seemingly so insignificant in the world's view?

The basic essence of temperance is *self-control*, which has two aspects: (1) *resistance* to influences from others, and (2) *restraint* from being overcome by impulses. Resistance to outside forces is essential in being temperate because the world will always provide ample reasons to tempt people away from the temperate path, and ample excuses to justify intemperate ways. No matter what the peer pressure, no matter what everybody else is doing, no matter what supposed scholarly rationalizations are given, temperate people will remain fixed on an inner source of strength. Those who pay the price of not going along with the vices of society will purchase for themselves personal maturity as so aptly summarized by Rudyard Kipling in his poem "If":

> If you can keep your head when all about you
> Are losing theirs and blaming it on you;
> . . . you'll be a Man, my son!

When I speak of resistance to outside forces I am not advocating becoming a social recluse or so prideful in your self-centered self-sufficiency that "you don't need anybody." I am advocating that you choose carefully what you allow into your life, what books you read, what songs you listen to, what images you see, and who you associate with. If you fill your world with intemperate influences, your thoughts, feelings, and actions will eventually be devoid of temperance. Those influences will, in time, betray you.

> One night in late October,
> When I was far from sober,
> Returning with my load with manly pride,
> My feet began to stutter,
> So I lay down in the gutter,
>
> And a pig came near and lay down by my side;
> A lady passing by was heard to say:
> "You can tell a man who boozes,
> By the company he chooses."
> And the pig got up and slowly walked away.
> —from "Judged by the Company One Keeps," author unknown

The second aspect of self-control is a restraint to the inner drives, forces, and passions that lead us away from transcendent purity. In other words, temperance is rising above the self-centered animalistic nature. Because this lower nature (Plato's "appetite," Freud's "id," the apostle Paul's "flesh") is nevertheless *human* nature, much inner strength and determination is needed to keep it under control. It is so easy for this side of nature to slip out. I know, because there are times when I really struggle with being temperate.

An ironic example of this occurred during the time I was writing an earlier draft of this chapter. After spending the day in my office writing about temperance I came home and gave into my kids' pleas to cook pancakes—my special, old Pennsylvania Dutch recipe (at least that's what it says on the bag). I served up the pancakes, but the syrup had run dry and I needed to open a new bottle. *No problem*, I thought. Big problem I found out, because I couldn't get the lid off of the top of the new bottle. After several minutes of fruitless struggle, I got frustrated and eventually slammed the plastic bottle down on the counter. Big mistake, because the bottle exploded and sticky syrup was everywhere! "Gee, Dad, that was neat," said my son Karston, who was three years old at the time. He then added that he didn't think I could get syrup in so many places, so far apart, in such a short period of time. I sure felt like a fool. What a great role model I provided for the kids! And *I'm* going to tell others about temperance? Months later I was still finding syrup in odd places about our house. What a mess! That's the problem when you let your guard down and intemperance rises to the surface: Big, far-reaching messes are created in a short period of time that often take a long period of time to clean up.

My guess is that a lot of people are frustrated by their inability to get a grip on their tempers, bad habits, and indulgences. Many probably lead to stickier situations than syrupy dining areas. How can you get on top of that lower nature? I have found two key factors toward developing the personal restraint needed to be temperate.

First, intemperance often involves a lack of rationality. In other words, we act before we think; we react without thinking. The tongue works overtime, and the brain is sleeping on the job. Intemperance is like letting go of the reins of a high-spirited horse. To control that horse means taking control of those reins. It is interesting that the word *reins* refers to not only the leather straps attached to the bit of a horse, but historically has carried the meaning of "feelings and affections." Being temperate requires pulling tight the reins of unchecked emotionality, but also giving proper room for appropriate feelings to be expressed. In both cases the "rider" must be a *thoughtful* person; reason controls the feelings and actions, not the other way around. Once you take control of that high-spirited horse, you'll be able to go far. But you must let reason, not the emotional horse, be in charge.

> Have ye vices that ask a destroyer?
> Or passions that need your control?
> Let Reason become your employer,
> And your body ruled by your soul.
> Fight on, though ye bleed in the trial,
> Resist with all strength that ye may,
> Ye may conquer Sin's host by denial;
> For "Where there's a will there's a way."
> —from "Where There's a Will There's a Way" by Eliza Cook

What are the attributes of this way of reason that enables one to master her or his lower nature? I propose a *Rule of Four*:

1. *Forbearance*: Temperate people patiently restrain their passions, not letting their impulses control them, in spite of justifiable provocation.
2. *Forbiddance*: The temperate do not permit impure thoughts to dominate their thinking, censoring the temptations before they gain a foothold in their minds.

3. *Forethought*: Temperate individuals think before they act and consider the long-term implications and consequences rather than merely the short-term costs and benefits.
4. *Forgiveness*: Temperance gives up the injustices, resentments, and angers that only serve to dispel the inner quietness and lead to harm.

The second key toward developing personal restraint is spiritual. I have found that the more I read the Scriptures, pray, and attend to God, the less of a problem I have being self-controlled. Temperance is not an end in itself; it is a means to purity. As we purify our minds we are better able to clarify our vision of God. "Blessed are the *pure* in heart, for they will *see* God" (Matt. 5:8). How blessed, yes, how happy are those whose lives are tempered by the Spirit of God so that they may see their Creator! By letting God, rather than earthly pleasures, shape their lives, they lose it all (temporally) but gain it all (eternally).

> How happy is he born and taught
> That serveth not another's will;
> Whose armour is his honest thought
> And simple truth his utmost skill;
>
> Whose passions not his masters are;
> Whose soul is still prepared for death,
> Not tied unto the world with care
> Of public fame, or private breath;
>
> Who God doth late and early pray
> More of His grace than gifts to lend;
> And entertains the harmless day
> With a well-chosen book or friend; . . .
>   —from "Character of a Happy Life" by Sir H. Walton

A Tree of Life

> He is like a tree planted by streams of water, which yields its fruit in season and whose leaf does not wither. Whatever he does prospers. (Ps. 1:3)

Yad vashem. In Hebrew these words are what God promised to give to eunuchs who would follow Him: a "place and a name"

(Isa. 56:5). *Place*—where I am, my roots, my aspirations, my dwelling in the universe. *Name*—who I am, my self-identity, my character, my role in eternity. In Jerusalem today there is a hill where the words *place* and *name* have a special meaning. For on this hillside sets an institution known as Yad Vashem.

Yad Vashem was established in 1953 to honor the martyrs and heroes of the holocaust. Leading up to and away from Yad Vashem is a path surrounded by some specially planted trees. These trees were planted in the memory of and, when possible, by people called "Righteous Christians"—those individuals who at the risk or sacrifice of their own lives saved Jews from the Nazi death camps. Only carob trees, whose leaves do not wither in the harsh climactic conditions of Jerusalem, are used. Those trees symbolize the lives of people who, like those spoken of in the first Psalm, do not walk in the counsel of the wicked and therefore bear the fruit of godliness, whose "leaf does not wither." It is significant that the pods of these trees are what both John the Baptist (what *locusts* referred to) and the prodigal son survived on. Furthermore, because the seeds from the carob tree are of nearly uniform weight, most authorities believe that it was carob seeds that were used in scales to measure gold, pearls, and diamonds in the ancient world (the word *carat* derives from the Greek word for carob fruit). How appropriate that trees that provided a measure of precious material qualities have become the measure of precious spiritual qualities. This living memorial of trees is known as "The Avenue of the Righteous."

Who are these righteous folk? The most striking feature of their biographies is that they are primarily ordinary people—laborers, office workers, police officers, schoolteachers, etc., who performed extraordinary deeds. What motivated these "average" people to do something so heroic? Desire for fame or fortune? Not at all. In fact, the committee that searches for worthy candidates considers only those where a purity of motive can be established. To those for whom trees are planted, the roots of their actions must be found within a moral and spiritual *rootedness* that resisted the uncontrollable fury and hatred of Nazi evil.

When I was a child, my father dug up several evergreen trees and transplanted them to different locations on our property. Weeks later it became apparent that some of those trees were turning into "everbrowns" as they began to dry up and wither away. The problem was that the root structure of the transplanted trees was inadequate, not allowing them to grow in a different area. Without a proper root structure, there was no growth and life began to ebb away.

We can see a similar effect in the lives of people. I worked for a few years in psychiatric settings for troubled children. Most of them were sent to the clinics because of the trouble they got into at school, with the law, etc. While there were many differences among these children, there was one factor that was quite common: lack of a stable, two-parent home. Without the roots of two loving parents these kids had great difficulty adapting to different settings. Unlike the first Psalm, whatever they did failed to lead to prosperity. Their lives ran out of control because they hadn't learned self-control. Perhaps they weren't shown self-control in their broken homes. Maybe there just wasn't a parent around when she or he was really needed. Whatever the case may be, lack of good roots in the family stunted their growth, morally and spiritually. Break up the family and you'll unleash in society kids, and eventually adults, lacking temperance.

Children, like trees, need roots. They also, like trees, need a *proper balance* of that which is necessary for growth. Trees grow best where there is a proper balance of nutrients, water, and sunlight. Take the nutrient nitrogen, for example: Not enough nitrogen or too much nitrogen can prevent the tree from bearing fruit. Extremes of deficiencies and excesses, likewise, hold back people's ability to produce fruit in their lives. Philosophers from Aristotle to Confucius have extolled the virtues of the "Golden Mean," proposing that the virtuous course is midway between the extremes of deficiency and excess. Take eating, for example: The extremes of starving yourself or stuffing yourself are both harmful to your body. When people put into practice habits of moderation, a balanced lifestyle results and bears the fruit of temperance. Adam and Eve lost their self-control and ate the forbidden fruit. When we forbid losing control, we will eat of the fruit of the tree of life in God's garden—the truly balanced diet.

Fruit trees bear their fruit in season, a fact noted in the first Psalm. It takes time for the fruit to be produced. I've seen recent converts to Christianity think that just because they've given their lives to God, all those bad habits in their lives—the temper with a short fuse, the tongue too quick to speak, the credit card bill too high— will shortly disappear. Many recent converts become frustrated as they continue to struggle with their intemperances, and some even fall away from the faith. It's as if salvation and sanctification are thought to be one in the same and problems in the latter area must be indicative of something wrong in the former area. However, while salvation is a crossing over of the bottomless chasm between death and life, sanctification is the daily process of growing and walking in that life. The walk of temperance takes time. Temperance is not one day's achievement; it is a lifelong walk that makes it more possible that in each succeeding day the achievement of temperance is more frequent. The challenge of temperance is to be strong enough to walk the distance. Grow in the knowledge of temperate ways, promise to yourself and God to keep yourself pure, and commit for the long haul. If you do, you will be like the tree planted by streams of water.

> Whose woods these are I think I know . . .
> The woods are lovely, dark and deep.
> But I have promises to keep,
> And miles to go before I sleep,
> And miles to go before I sleep.
> —from "Stopping by Woods on a Snowy Evening" by Robert Frost

Withered Trees

> . . . and because they had no root, they dried up and withered away. (Matt. 13:6)

Reason, moderation, and roots combine to provide a foundation for a moral and spiritual self-control that leads a person to the peace of inner purity. That purity is polluted, however, when the foundation is disturbed and the balanced self-control is thrown out of equilibrium. Most of the imbalances of intemperance can be found in two areas: under-control and over-control.

The most glaring, obvious acts of intemperance are usually found in *under-control*. I once had an opportunity to teach a Sunday school class on the Seven Deadly Sins. While putting the class topics together I noticed that each of these seven sins (first grouped together by Pope Gregory in the sixth century A.D.) had at its root intemperance. Consider the lack of control found in each of these sins:

1. Anger: "resentful or revengeful displeasure"—an inability to control your temper
2. Covetousness: "greedy, grasping, taking without thought of others' needs, desiring more than what is needed"—the out-of-control desire to acquire

3. Envy: "resentful dislike and discontent because of another's advantages"—unable to control the insecurity of what you have in life
4. Gluttony: "voraciously devouring more than you need"—loss of the ability to stop eating, drinking, or taking drugs
5. Lust: "excessive desire to fulfill sensual pleasures"—losing yourself to pleasure
6. Pride: "overbearing and high opinion of oneself"—unable to control how good you feel about yourself
7. Sloth: "laziness, idleness, disinclination to exert oneself"—lack of personal discipline

I have also noticed that the lack of control evident in the seven sins revolves around the pleasure principle. In anger and envy, something or someone is inhibiting the ability to feel pleasure; in covetousness, gluttony, and lust, getting more means more pleasure; in pride, more is pleasurable; in sloth, conversely, less is pleasurable. Pleasure is usually the motive that moves people to under-control. But, how many people given to such motivations ever find lasting satisfaction, a genuine peace of mind? When people sell out their love of God for their love of pleasure, no lasting happiness can be found. In fact, I've only seen people who, in their sorrows over their excesses, change their lifestyles and embrace temperate ways who truly find lasting peace of mind. This was aptly penned by Robert Browning Hamilton.

> I walked a mile with Pleasure;
> She chattered all the way,
> But left me none the wiser
> For all she had to say.
>
> I walked a mile with Sorrow
> And ne'er a word said she;
> But oh, the things I learned from her
> When Sorrow walked with me!
>
> —from "Along the Road"

On the other hand, *over-control* is the equally dangerous opposite road to impurity. It is applying too much restraint of one's desires and emotions, rather than giving them their proper expression. Thus, physical love is inhibited by excessive prudishness, fear of being fat leads to the unhealthy self-starvation of anorexia, and proper use of money is negated by stinginess. The roots of over-control are usually found in insecurity. For example, prudishness may be the result of feeling ashamed of sexuality or feeling poorly about your physical attractiveness. Anorexia can be caused by an insecure need to feel accepted (e.g., "Thin is in") or a reaction to a lack of control in your life (e.g., past abuse or parental domination). Stingy people are often terribly afraid of being without money—money is their security blanket.

Deficiencies of temperance are so common that great efforts are made to justify them. Sometimes biology comes to the rescue, like legitimizing lack of sexual purity by appealing to the habits of lower animals to advocate lower morals through evolutionary explanations (e.g., "We are genetically programmed to be sexually promiscuous"). At other times, the rationalizations are given a sociological or psychological framework, such as blaming all troubles on the environment (e.g., societies, not individuals, are the ultimate roots of problems). Intemperances are cloaked under privacies, protected under "liberties," and even extolled as acts of "freedom" or "self-expression." However, no matter what the *excuse*, the virtuous person will find a *reason* for choosing the path that leads to inner purity. According to the words of Jesus Christ, this is not a road that most people will choose: "Enter through the narrow gate. For wide is the gate and broad is the way that leads to destruction, and many enter through it. But small is the gate and narrow the road that leads to life and only a few find it" (Matt. 7:13–14).

When one chooses the green tree of temperance in the forest of intemperances, when a person chooses to travel the way that most will not tread, the ultimate consequence will be a spiritual peace of mind and inner purity that are eternally priceless.

> Two roads diverged in a yellow wood,
> and sorry I could not travel both
> And be one traveler, long I stood
> And looked down as far as I could.
>
> Two roads diverged in a wood, and I -
> I took the one less traveled by,
> And that has made all the difference.
> —from "The Road Not Taken" by Robert Frost

Be different. Be temperate. It will make all the difference!

Temperance . . .

1. bridles the passion of *courage*, restraining those who dare to be great from daring too greatly;
2. demonstrates a *just* way of dealing with self and others, a self-control, not a selfish control;
3. motivates a person toward inner purity, making clearer a guiding light to the *wise*;
4. helps the *faithful* see God through the purity of their hearts;
5. checks the tendencies toward gullibility and skepticism, ensuring that *hopes* are neither groundless or ground down;
6. forces a person to look inward, making it more natural for *lovers* to look at the inner qualities of others and not to be deceived by the often superficial charms of attractiveness;

. . . the growing contentment of creating balanced self-control.

faith A transcencing trust:
spiritually, in the
apprehension of and
adherence to God's truth;
psychologically, in the confident
belief and reliance in a person

Chapter 6

Blueprint for Life

And he made the robe of the ephod of woven work all of blue.
—Exod. 39:22

SHORTLY AFTER KATHLEEN AND I WERE MARRIED, WE DECIDED TO SAVE A GOOD portion of our income in order to buy a house. As the funds for our downpayment grew, we began to search more earnestly for a house. We looked at a number of different houses, but we could not find anything to our liking. Eventually, we came to the conclusion that building a home would give us a better chance of getting a home to our liking and in the right price range.

We wrote to many builders and only one firm went out of their way to work with us. We were invited to their main office, where we met a man skilled in drawing up plans for houses. It was an exciting time for us; we could design any type of home we wanted. Kathleen and I talked a lot about the type of home we desired to live in, shared our ideas with the architect, and then we waited to see what our ideas would look like on paper. We saw the first plans for our home, made some changes, and then agreed with the builder to have the home built. It took several months before the house was finished. During that time, we enjoyed driving out to our property to check out the latest progress.

Once, shortly after the basement was finished, our son Christian, who was two at the time, looked at the concrete hole in the ground and asked if we were going to live in a barge! We had to explain to him that it takes time for the full vision of the blueprint plans to become a reality. As I look back on those days of building our house, I see a strong similarity to another building process, one that the Master Builder is working out in our lives through a blueprint called faith.

The blueprint of our home was based on knowledge: the knowledge of the architect in drawing plans, and the knowledge of what we wanted to be drawn into those plans. Contrary to the opinion of many, faith is also a blueprint based on *knowledge*. Faith is a living relationship. How can you have a relationship with someone you don't know? To put your faith in a person or in God demands that your thinking be at its clearest, its most informed, and its most prudent. The cost of trusting yourself to the wrong source is steep. The more you trust in another, the deeper the wound if that trust is betrayed. If you are to trust *in* someone, you must use the fullest of your *in*tellect; you must know who you trust in. Faith is always a trust *in*, an *in*formed trust.

While faith demands the utmost of your reasoning abilities, if it goes no further than the limits of your intellect, it is a sham. Faith requires something more than your intellectual assent. There are times when Kathleen will give me a puzzled look and say, "What are you doing?"

Sometimes I'll smile and just say, "Trust me!" I can smile easily because I know she will. My wife's trust in me goes beyond what she knows of me. How comforting I find her trust in me. So too, if the only evidence of God is what I can know, then God is limited by my intellect and is no God after all—only my idolatrous creation. Nor can God merely be the One who inhabits what I do not know. If that were so, then as I grow in knowledge, the God of the unknowable would shrink and I would become more the creator and God more the creation. God, to be truly God, must be knowable but also unknowable. Faith must embrace both the knowable and the unknowable, that which makes sense and that which is insensible, that which engages the intellect and that which *transcends* the intellect.

It took time for the blueprint of our home to be transformed into the house that we now live in. Yet Kathleen and I were confident after signing a contract that even though our house was not a physical reality, what we saw in the blueprint was a reality and we were going to live in what was drawn on a piece of paper. My skeptical friends only want to make a contract with God *after* the house is built and they can see it and feel it. Just as our architect required us to trust in him *before* the house was built, so too a contract with God requires beforehand a trust in Him. That's why in Hebrews 11:6 it is written, "But without faith it is impossible to please and be satisfactory to Him." Faith must take on us a journey from the here and now (concrete reality) to the there and then (abstract reality). If your foot is stuck in concrete reality, you'll never be able to travel with God.

Part of the transformation process from a paper to a wood-and-brick home involved choosing certain details. One of those details was choosing the interior color scheme. Since Kathleen and I are blue lovers, we had no difficulty agreeing on what the inside of our house would look like—blue is everywhere! Blue appears to be a favorite color of God also. Why else would God instruct Moses to make the covering of the priests' attire to be "wholly blue"? It's interesting that when the Hebrew tabernacle was being moved in the desert, God instructed the Israelites to cover most of the sacred articles in blue cloths (see Num. 4). God also covers us with blue—the sky—and surrounds us with the blueness of the seas. There is something sacred about that. As a child, I loved blue so much that I would reach up into the air and try to grab hold of some of that pretty blue sky. I would open my hands and, of course, no blue. A similar attempt with water led to the same result. *Why*, I thought as a child, *can I not get hold of that blue that so obviously exists*? Scientific explanations aside, I realized that there is a reality that you cannot firmly hold in your hands. God is a reality that many people cannot get a grip on either. They wave their hands in the air, grasp for something they cannot attain in their misguided attempts, and then tell others there is nothing there. Through faith we understand that there are a multiplicity of realities. "True blue" believers see God where others see nothing.

> When I think of God's great universe
> With its vast expanse of sky,
> And of those who can roam from sea to sea
> Without a thought of why
> This wondrous joy is given to them
> By a God so kind and true,
> I wonder if they are quite as glad
> As I, for my "Patch of Blue." . . .
> —from "My Patch of Blue" by Mary Newland Carson

The Ring of True

> And the son said to him, Father I have sinned against heaven and in your sight; I am no longer worthy to be called your son! But the father said to his bond servants, Bring quickly the best robe and put it on him; and give him a ring for his hand and sandals for his feet. (Luke 15:21–22)

I love the parable of the prodigal son. I've been that son. I moved away from my childlike belief in God to an "educated" agnosticism. I was too smart to believe. But in 1977, while working on my doctorate in psychology, I realized how dumb I was to not believe in the One who has spread the heavens above my head, the earth beneath my feet, and His Spirit within my soul. Like the prodigal son, I found that when I no longer believed, my Father still believed in me and had a place for me in His home. I find it significant that the prodigal son's father put a ring on his finger. The ring symbolizes unending—the circle has no beginning or end—fidelity, devotion, and trust. That's certainly what the father demonstrated to the prodigal son by putting a ring on his finger. Many years ago Kathleen—my faithful, devoted, and trustworthy wife—heard a man by the name of Dave Roever tell another story about a ring of faithfulness. Only this story was not a parable, but a true testimony to the power of transcending trust.

Dave was performing his normal duties on board a gunboat in Vietnam when disaster struck. A white-phosphorus grenade he was holding beside his head inadvertently exploded. The effect on Dave was devastating: The chemical released by the grenade burned the skin off much of his body, his right ear was obliterated, the right side of his nose was gone, and only one finger on his right hand was still firmly attached. There was a large hole in his chest, and much of his body was reduced to charred skin interrupted by patches of exposed bone. Throughout his long and painful recovery in being removed from Vietnam to Japan, and eventually back to America, Dave was haunted by a feared devastation of a different nature: Would his wife, Brenda, remain faithful to this battered and broken body of a man she sent off to war?

Dave could not be encouraged by a scene played out before him on the hospital ward in Texas. A married woman had come into the ward of grossly disfigured soldiers to identify her husband. When she found him, shocked at his appearance, she told him that he would be a disgrace to be seen with, removed the wedding ring from her finger, dropped it between his feet on the hospital bed, and walked away. That soldier died sometime later, though the real deathblow probably came in the hospital, rather than the battle-field. A while after this incident, Brenda came to see her man. Dave's heart leapt for joy when Brenda bent down, kissed him, and said, "Welcome home, Davey. I love you." The ring stayed put.

Two disfigured soldiers in hospital beds were taught different lessons about faith by their wives. To one wife, the ring slid off her finger easily; to another, it was impossible to remove the ring. To their husbands, the fidelity of their wives—symbolized by what they did with their wedding rings—made all the difference in the world. Dave Roever became a traveling emissary of God, sharing his Christian testimony of hope, love, and faith. And Brenda? She's with her man because she's with her God. A remarkable story. Yet, to all partners in faith something remarkable is happening in their lives.

When you trust in another person, when you believe in God, *you are changed by your trusting*. Brenda believed in Dave, and Dave was empowered by that trust. I'm sure that Dave found it even easier to believe in his wife. That's the amazing thing about the power of faith: The more you are trusted in, the easier you find it to trust. Furthermore, I have found that people who trust readily are more readily trusted in. There is a power of faith that changes those who share in faith. I've also seen remarkable changes in people's lives when they move from disbelief to trusting in God. It becomes so much more difficult for them to depart from truth-fulness. When you open your heart in faith to God, who is "the way, the *truth*, and the life" (John 14:6), truth pours in and honesty, trustworthiness, sincerity, and loyalty spill out of a person's life. The faithful touch of the Master's hand has the power to change the lives of those He touches.

> T'was battered and scarred, and the auctioneer
> Thought it scarcely worth his while
> To waste much time on the old violin,
> But held it up with a smile:
> "What am I bidden, good folks," he cried,
> "Who'll start the bidding for me?"
> "A dollar, a dollar"; then, "Two!" "Only two?
> Two dollars, and who'll make it three?
> Three dollars, once; three dollars, twice;

Going for three—" But no,
From the room, far back, a gray-haired man
Came forward and picked up the bow;
Then, wiping the dust from the old violin,
And tightening the loose strings,
He played a melody pure and sweet
As a caroling angel sings.

The music ceased, and the auctioneer,
With a voice that was quiet and low,
Said: "What am I bid for the old violin?"
And he held it up with the bow.
"A thousand dollars, and who'll make it two?
Two thousand! And who'll make it three?
Three thousand, once, three thousand, twice,
And going, and gone," said he.
The people cheered, but some of them cried,
"We do not quite understand
What changed its worth." Swift came the reply:
"The touch of a master's hand."

And many a man with life out of tune,
And battered and scarred with sin,
Is auctioned cheap to the thoughtless crowd,
Much like the old violin.
A "mess of pottage," a glass of wine;
A game—and he travels on.
He is "going" once, and "going" twice,
He's "going" and almost "gone."
But the Master comes, and the foolish crowd
Never can quite understand
The worth of a soul and the change that's wrought
By the touch of the Master's hand.
    —from "The Touch of the Master's Hand" by Myra Brooks Welch

When Kathleen and I were engaged, she lived in Oklahoma and I resided in Iowa. I received a call from her one night, and she told me that she had gone to the jewelry store and picked out a wedding ring for me. On my next visit, she said we would go to the store and, if I liked it, she'd buy it for me. The day arrived when I could drive down to see my loved one, and Kathleen couldn't wait to show me the ring she picked out. So we drove to the jewelry store, and Kathleen—with that impish grin of hers—told me she wasn't going to tell me which of the dozens of rings she had chosen. She told me that she'd buy any ring I picked while the jewelry store clerk amusedly smiled. What a change in expression came over his face when I picked a simple gold band with a silver cross etched on the outside. He, with eyes bulging in surprise, informed me that the ring I had picked out was the same one Kathleen had reserved for purchase previously. How could she know, with all the choices, which ring I would choose? Dumb luck? No, Kathleen knew a lot about that uncomplicated guy she was going to marry, and that gave her the confidence to do what she did. I learned a good lesson about faith in God in that jewelry store.

People find it a seeming contradiction to believe that freedom of choice and God's all-knowing nature are compatible. In other words, if God knows everything I am going to do, do I really have any freedom of choice? God's people are called His chosen or elect. What does it matter, then, what people say or do if it all is determined beforehand by God? This seeming paradoxical state of affairs is not as much of a contradiction as it appears to be on the surface. In Kathleen's knowledge of who I am, she rightly predicted which choice I would make in a jewelry store. I, however, was under no compulsion to make that choice. I chose a ring that I did not have the slightest hint that Kathleen had previously picked out. So much more the case spiritually. God, in His unlimited knowledge, knows all the choices we will make in life. To believe in God, however, is a choice that we have the freedom to choose. God knows who are His, but we are under no compulsion to choose to follow Him. Even though Kathleen had a good idea which ring I would choose, I still had to make that choice in order to wear the ring. Even though God has a perfect idea of who will choose to follow Him, we must still make that *choice* if we are to receive His salvation.

The ring: symbol of trust, sign of faithfulness. Hold up a ring before your eyes and see eternity (no beginning or end), and behold unity (oneness). Trust in God and peer more clearly into eternity. Believe in the One who is life and you will live forever as one with God.

Death, be not proud, though some have called thee
Mighty and dreadful, for thou art not so;
For those whom thou think'st thou dost overthrow
Die not, poor Death, nor yet canst thou kill me.
From rest and sleep, which but thy pictures be,
Much pleasure; then from thee much more must flow,
And soonest our best men with thee do go,

Rest of their bones, and soul's delivery.
Thou'rt slave to fate, chance, kings, and desperate men,
And dost with poison, war, and sickness dwell;
And poppy or charms can make us sleep as well
And better than thy stroke; why swell'st thou then?
One short sleep past, we wake eternally,
And death shall be no more; Death, thou shalt die.
—from "Death, Be Not Proud" by John Donne

Trust Rust

> Your gold and silver are completely rusted through, and their rust will be a testimony against you and it will devour your flesh as if it were fire. (James 5:3)

Have you ever asked about a person and been told, "You can trust her. Her word is gold!"? When I'm told that someone's word is gold it means to me that she or he speaks truthfully, sincerely, and is someone I can depend on. I once knew someone that I thought was truthful, sincere, and dependable. But, as people came to me and told me of things this person said and did behind my back, I lost my trust in that person. There have also been times in my life where my truthfulness, sincerity, and dependability have fallen short of God's standard. As I've thought of those sins, my faith in myself has plummeted. Where there is lack of faith, a cancer grows—a psychological, social, and spiritual cancer that I call *trust rust*.

Psychologically, trust rust is found in lies, deceptions, and instability. You cannot trust that unfaithful people's feelings are sincere and genuine. Beware of their pretentious and affected displays of empathy and concern for others: Overdone emotionality is often a symptom of underdone sincerity. Unfaithful people would rather do things behind your back than before your face. One of their main motivations will be to cover up their true intents. Rationalizations, excuses, and euphemistic language will be heavily employed. Thus, adultery becomes an "affair of the heart," treachery is transformed into an "act of conscience," and betrayal is said to be "prudent action."

A lot of unfaithful people hide behind a cloak of intellectual skepticism. Faithless people may be quite intelligent. Sometimes the high IQs are only exceeded by inflated egos. Their arrogance will be so high that they will be unable to believe in someone or something beyond their reasoning abilities. They will mock the "blind faithful" but are too proud to recognize the blindness of their doubting. At other times, sharp criticisms and mocking gibes are coverups for self-doubts. Those who readily see what's wrong with others usually have a lot of wrong going on inside themselves. Don't be surprised to find the most striking examples of lack of faith in seminaries and departments of religious studies on college campuses, where faith has been transferred from one three letter word, *God*, to another, *ego*. Their pride in being "properly skeptical inquirers" will blind them to the truth, even denying that truth is possible. There is no room for God in a mind filled with itself.

> Of old our fathers' God was real,
> Something they almost saw,
> Which kept them to a stern ideal
> And scourged them into awe . . .
>
> Now Hell has wholly boiled away
> And God become a shade.
> There is no place for him to stay
> In all the world he made.
> —from "Exit God" by Gamaliel Bradford

Socially, mistrust will eat away the bonds that keep people together. Several years ago a man confided in me that he had betrayed his wife in an act of adultery. He said he eventually told his wife, but their marriage was "just not the same anymore." He told me that it was just a one-night affair and he couldn't understand why his wife couldn't get over it. I told him that he was correct in the fact that his marriage wasn't the same anymore. Once you break a sacred vow by sexual infidelity you never again have a union of perfect fidelity. Yes, we can forgive others for their inevitable failings of faith, but there are some acts that can crack the foundations of any relationship. In marriage, adultery is just such an act. The greater the amount of time and effort put into building a faith relationship, the greater the impact of its breaking, and the harder it will be to rebuild it. When trust is small, little is lost when the trust is broken. However, the more you invest in believing in someone, the more you are likely to lose when that belief is betrayed.

I heard a woman say, when asked about the sexual infidelities of a world leader, that we should not make a big deal about it. To justify her answer she mentioned a particular country where this is much more acceptable and "nobody gets real bothered by such stuff." Hmm. What she is really pointing out is that there is a country where marriage is neither that important or sacred if it is so easy and acceptable to betray your spouse. You can tell how much people truly trust in one another by how much they work to nourish and safeguard that trust, not by how easily they can forsake their fidelity. Those who find it difficult to bestow trust, find it easy to betray trust.

When I talk about marriage in some of my classes, I sometimes use expressions such as "a sacred union" or "a spiritual covenant." When I use those expressions, I get a few snickering expressions and some rolling eyes. Marriage is "just a piece of paper" I have been told by some students. These reactions are a symptom of a society that has *lost touch with God*. If you look at Western civilization over the last half of the twentieth century, you find a tripling of births out of wedlock. Marriage is set apart from God, and inevitably bearing children is set apart from marriage. Where respect for God wanes, there will follow a lack of respect for relationships—especially those once considered sacred. Where people don't blush at sin and are not shocked by vices, they have lost their virtuous calling and cannot hear the voice of God. Where faith in God is easily mocked, marriage is lightly regarded.

Unfortunately, it is often those people who are supposed to be representatives of God—the clergy—who do the most damage in weakening people's faith in God. There is a common route these folks take: Water down the Bible. Kathleen and I once went to a church where there was a guest sermon. This "minister of God," a philosophy professor, he carefully explained, spent twenty minutes explaining why the Bible is not true before finally coming to the point that there actually were a certain number of columns in a temple that the apostle John wrote about in his gospel. Well, hallelujah and shout amen! Now that's a message to take to the world! Hey friend, did you know that there really were ——— (I forget exactly how many were said) columns in a temple that's now a pile of dust? Wow, that'll really change someone's life!

While listening to that "sermon" I leaned over to my wife and said something she was also thinking: "If almost none of this is true, what are we doing here?" If I was Satan, I'd sneak in as many folks as possible to water down God's words. I'd get churches and denominations to be more concerned about the praise that comes from people than from God. And, I'd make sure that the foundation of people's belief in God is so weakened, that it would be easy to break people of their faithfulness to God.

Break people of their faithfulness to God and anything is possible. Well, Satan has been doing that for centuries and will continue that strategy until the end of the world. Through it all, however, there will always be those people who can open the pages of a special book and see God. Their lives will be changed forever.

> Last eve I passed beside a blacksmith's door,
> And heard the anvil ring the vesper chime;
> Then, looking in, I saw upon the floor
> Old hammers, worn with beating years of time.
>
> "How many anvils have you had," said I,
> "To wear and batter all these hammers so?"
> "Just one," said he, and then, with twinkling eye,
> "The anvil wears the hammers out, you know."
>
> And so, thought I, the anvil of God's Word,
> For ages skeptic blows have beat upon;
> Yet, though the noise of falling blows was heard,
> The anvil is unharmed—the hammers gone.
> —from "The Anvil—God's Word," author unknown

Faith . . .

1. provides the *courageous* a strong rock to stand on, while every grain of the sand of unfaithfulness gives a coward a reason for not standing firm;
2. motivates people to be *just* in their dealings with others through their experience with the wholly just God of eternity;
3. gives birth to *wisdom,* because before you can be wise, you must believe that you can be wise;
4. reveals that the holy God of the universe is the essence of purity, whose Spirit empowers the growth of *temperance*;
5. declares that when there is every reason in the world to give up *hope*, there is every reason in heaven to continue to hope;
6. is the inspiration of *love*; lack of faith is love's expiration;

. . . becoming one with people and God through steadfast trust.

Hope *A continual looking forward to the actualization of desire*

Chapter 7

The Middle-Child Syndrome

And so faith, hope, love abide, these three . . . 1 Cor. 13:13

I WAS DISCUSSING THE THREE THEOLOGICAL VIRTUES IN CLASS, AND A STUDENT raised her hand and exclaimed, "I can see the importance of faith and love, but isn't hope just a part of faith and love and unnecessarily distinguished from the other two virtues?"

My first thought, fortunately not expressed, was, "Honey, if you ever tried to get a book published, then you'd learn about hope!" Upon further reflection, however, I understood what she meant. Hope it seems "just don't get any respect." Hope is like a middle child, caught between the high-achieving faith sibling and the pampered, last-but-certainly-not-least sibling called love. Even the color of hope, indigo, defined as a deep violet-blue, seems to be swallowed up by the colors of love (violet) and faith (blue). To many, hope is like a conjunction, interchangeable with *and* in talking about faith and love. However, it is clear from the apostle Paul's letter to the Corinthians that hope is distinguishable from faith and love. What are its distinguishing characteristics?

In his letter to the Colossians, Paul makes a case that both faith and love are rooted in hope (see Col. 1:4–5). That's one of the primary attributes of hope: It provides its possessor *roots*. When you have the roots of hope in your life you can hold onto your faith and love through the difficult times, because you have a deep-rooted reason for believing and loving. I see this in the lives of my children. They were born into this world utterly dependent on other people to meet their needs for survival. As my wife and I consistently attended to their needs, they began to learn of trust and love. Crucially, they began to learn of the virtue of hope. Our consistency in meeting their needs gave them reason to believe that, even if their needs were not immediately met—whether wet diaper or the need for wet nourishment—they eventually would be taken care of. In other words, they learned; "My needs will eventually be satisfied. If not now, they will."

Faith and love may seem to be hidden and hard to find in present circumstances. But when we learn to hope, we can *stretch* our faith and love beyond the mystery of the moment. For faith and love to be vital forces in a person's life they have to project in the future. Only through hope can that be done. Only hopeful people can truly trust and love others and God. Hope carries you into the future, giving you strength to hold onto the faith and love of the present day.

Hopeful people do not idly waste the hours, daydreaming of things to come. Instead, the conviction of genuine hope motivates the hoper to action. The color of hope is indi*go*, not indi*stop*. That's what people of genuine hope do: They *go* and *do*. For example, the surer the hope of those who believe in the gospel, the greater the likelihood they will go and tell others the good news. The more genuine the hope, the greater the likelihood it will be acted upon. Many hopes start as dreams that others may consider to be useless, childish fantasies. It is so easy for people to criticize and make fun of others' dreams. But where would the world be without people who *dare* to dream? Dreaming is not enough, however. The seed of dreams must be planted in the soil of action in order for genuine hope to sprout. This is a lesson that I learned well many years ago.

I was a single man and, like many unmarried folks, I dreamed of being married to someone who truly loved me. Since I was in my thirties, I often wondered if that dream would ever come true for me. One winter day I was surprised by an invitation from some good friends to come visit them and get together with some mutual friends. I accepted their invitation and flew down from my home in Iowa to theirs in Oklahoma. We had a wonderful get-together one evening, and I was particularly struck by my feelings for a friend of the opposite gender. The party was over, my friend left, and I was left with puzzling thoughts and feelings: *I really like Kathleen as a friend, but could it be more than that? . . . I don't want to ruin our friendship by blurting out something stupid. . . . What would she really see in me anyway? I probably have less than a 1 percent chance that our relationship could be more than it is.* For the remainder of the week in Tulsa with my host friends I struggled with my thoughts, feelings, and dreams.

Finally it was time to go back to Iowa, and my hosts had arranged for Kathleen to drive me to the airport. Here was my big chance to say what was on my heart. Do I dare say it? I initially chickened out, but then I finally realized that I couldn't live with myself if I didn't at least try. So right before getting out of the parked car at the airport I quickly blurted out, "I think I like you for more than a friend." Kathleen took off her sunglasses, stared at me with pupils dilated in shock, and was initially speechless. I needed to catch a plane so we walked into the airport chatting. What we said was mostly drowned out by my pounding heartbeat. We parted company and . . . she dumped me! A letter from me was unanswered. Days, then weeks, then months—no contact. Oh well, at least I tried.

Well, you probably figured I wouldn't tell a story like this unless there was a better ending. You're right. Nine months after our March encounter I came home to a letter from Kathleen asking if *I* would consider again our relationship. I couldn't believe what I was reading! I jumped up on my coffee table, did a dance, and my heart has been dancing ever since I married that beautiful lady. God gave me a soul mate and turned a dream that I thought was too good to ever be true into a marriage that is so good and so true. It still scares me to think what my life would be like if I didn't clumsily blurt out those words in a parked car. I learned that God will bless those who act on their dreams. So, I implore you:

O keep a place apart,
Within your heart,
For little dreams to go!
—from "Hold Fast Your Dreams" by Louise Driscoll

It took months before the seed I planted in Kathleen's heart bore fruit. God taught me that when you sow hope, you will only reap if you are *patient*. The earthly part of human nature wants its desires satisfied *now*. But to nurture the spiritual side, you must learn to be patient and wait. How childish to think that God should be at your every beck and call. We are to serve God; He is not our servant. Hopeful and spiritual folks will be a patient lot. Through the teacher of experience they learn to watch and wait and not give up their hopes. One of my favorite poets, "unknown" (right up there with "anonymous" in my book), put it well in "Don't Quit":

When things go wrong, as they sometimes will,
When the road you're trudging seems all up hill,
When the funds are low and the debts are high,
And you want to smile, but you have to sigh,
When care is pressing you down a bit,
Rest, if you must—but don't you quit!

Life is queer with its twists and turns,
As everyone of us sometimes learns,
And many a failure turns about
When he might have won had he stuck it out;
Don't give up, though the pace seems slow—
You might succeed with another blow.

Often when the goal is nearer than
It seems to a faint and faltering man,
Often the struggler has given up
When he might have captured the victor's cup.
And he learned too late, when the night slipped down,
How close he was to the golden crown.

Success is failure turned inside out—
The silver tint of the clouds of doubt—
And you never can tell how close you are,
It may be near when it seems afar;
So stick to the fight when you're hardest hit—
It's when things seem worst that you mustn't quit.

The Ship of Hope

She is like the merchant ships, bringing her food from afar. (Prov. 31:14)

Near Valley Forge, Pennsylvania, there stands the Chapel of the Four Chaplains. Hanging on the wall in that chapel is a painting of a sinking ship with four men, arms locked together, awaiting the slide into eternity. Behind that painting lies an inspiring story.

Ministers George Fox and Clark Poling, Rabbi Alexander Goode, and Catholic priest Fr. John Washington left New York harbor with 902 other men on the troop ship *SS Dorchester* during World War II, bound for Greenland. Nazi submarines were raising havoc with Allied convoys at that time, and the *Dorchester* was doomed to become part of the casualties of the war. Only one hundred and fifty miles from the shores of Greenland a Nazi torpedo slammed into the *Dorchester* and set her on a course to the sea bottom, as panicked men scrambled to save themselves. The rest of the convoy, under a power blackout, steamed on, leaving the *Dorchester* behind.

On to the chaotic deck scene of the greatly listing ship came the four chaplains, handing out lifejackets and directing men to the boat stations. With neither enough lifejackets nor lifeboat space the situation was becoming hopeless. And yet, in the midst of a sinking ship of hopeless men, the four chaplains raised up a lifeboat of hope of a different nature. The chaplains called words of strength to those around them while at the same time they gave up their only hopes of survival—their lifejackets—to other men. On a ship without a prayer, they stood on the deck, arms locked together, praying for others. On a chaotic, dying ship, other men joined them in prayer, finding peace and life in the hope of a new destination as the *Dorchester* found her way to God's harbor. One of the 230 survivors, John Ladd, called it, ". . . the finest thing I have ever seen or hope to see this side of heaven."

Human history is full of remarkable stories, and the story of the *Dorchester* is one of those stories that has long struck a chord in my heart. In one account of this story, a survivor remarked how struck he was in seeing a group of peaceful sailors and soldiers surrounding the four chaplains. How could such a serene scene occur in so desperate a situation? I believe the reason for this apparent contradiction is the fact that when the chaplains directed the men to the hope of God, that one of the predominant attributes of hope—*peace*—welled up inside these doomed casualties of war. No matter what storms there are in life, if you are on board the ship of hope, you will be able to sail through the roughest of seas. Through hope we learn that though storms in life are inevitable, and some are worse than others, when we keep our hearts firmly in the ship of hope we will be able to pass safely through. It is through hope that we learn:

> When some great sorrow, like a mighty river,
> Flows through your life with peace-destroying power,
> And dearest things are swept from sight forever,

Say to your heart each trying hour:
"This, too, shall pass away."
—from "This, Too, Shall Pass Away" by Lanta Wilson Smith

Perhaps because my father was in the navy, I've always had a fondness for stories about ships. As a child I used to like to build models of ships, particularly the old sailing ships. As an adult, I find there is much to learn about hope in consideration of sailing vessels.

Ships are built to sail in one direction: forward. That's what hope tells the human heart: Keep going *forward*. My wife often says to me that if you're not growing, your dying. How true that is. When you lose hope in a relationship, it dies. When an athletic team loses hope in winning, they lose. When people lose hope in their abilities, they give up. When hope perishes from the human soul, that soul dies. People are meant to hope. Look at God's creation and see that all life is going in one direction: forward. Plants grow into the future, not the past. People grow older, not younger. Ships are designed to sail the seas in the forward direction. People are designed to sail the seas of time in the hope heading.

It is amazing that large ships can be controlled by a small rudder, a fact spoken of in the third chapter of the Book of James (vs. 4). Imagine how ridiculous to build a sailing ship without one! Yet many people have the idea that hope is like a ship without a rudder—no guiding intellect at the helm. Hope, on the contrary, like the ship, requires guidance. When you are hopeful, you must *plan* where you are to go. Planning gives order to hope, hope orders planning. Planning requires information. The best plans are made with the best available information. Just as sailor's plans are informed by maps, compasses, technological data, and in the old days, by the positions of the stars, so too the hopeful manifest *informed* aspirations. For Christians the hope of salvation is a soundly informed hope rooted in the holy Scriptures.

Sometimes information comes that tells the captain of the ship to change course, the rudder must be moved. Hoping needs a *flexible* rudder too. I can hope that the batter at the plate will get a hit and win the game for my team. Should he strike out, then it's time to put my hope in the next batter, the next inning, the next game, or if you are rooting for the Brooklyn Dodgers, the next year. (Chicago Cub fans seem to take it a century at a time.) It is not that hope is so fickle; it is that hope is rooted in reality, not fantasy.

The story of Noah's ark has been told and retold in various forms for thousands of years, in hundreds of cultures. Unlike Noah's ship, which was grounded thousands of years ago, there is another sacred ship currently sailing. Its sailors are calling to those around them, like Noah, "Come in and avoid the coming destruction." This ship is called *The Ship of God*. The Holy Spirit fills its sails. It is piloted by Christ and was designed by His Father. Churches have been built with this symbolism in mind throughout the centuries. The long part of the church, between the principal entrance and the area at the opposite end around the pulpit or altar, is called the *nave*. This word is from the Latin root *navis*, meaning "ship." This is also where the English word *navy* comes from. Perhaps it would be better to say that those who believe in the hope of Christ's salvation are a part of God's navy, instead of army. Salvation Navy? The import of this is that the church is like a ship and those sailors who confess Christ but think they don't need the help of their fellow shipmates are often in for a rough time—and prone to get off the correct course. When we hope we help others hope, in turn our hopes our built up by the hopes of others. Hopers in Christ need to realize they are all, ultimately, to be on one ship—God's ship—and friendly companions therein. Shared hope will lead to companion*ship*. Furthermore, the shipmates share the same destination, and that knowledge is "food from afar" for those who hope in Christ.

Shipwrecks

> The floods cover them; they sank in the depths like a stone.
> (Exod. 15:5)

In Roman mythology, *Dis* was the god of the lower world. When you lose hope, you lose a life-giving virtue and descend to that *lower* world. You find that Roman god mentioned in much that characterizes the hopeless. Their disaffection, disappointment, discontentment, discouragement, disenchantment, dismay, disquiet, and distress become so dismal that they are disconsolate. As a consequence of their disillusionment, they become disagreeable, disbelieving, discordant, disputatious, and distrustful. Dispossessed of hope, they distance themselves from sources of life, dissociating from friends, dissembling their emotions, disturbing their thinking, and allow dissolute ways to become the norm as virtuous ways dissipate and moral standards are discarded. Hope will lift you up, loss of hope will pull you down. Beware of those things and people who would have you trade in the richness of indigo for the faded poverty of indi*gone*.

I have a skeptical friend who considers most hopeful people as hopelessly gullible. I agree that swallowing everything you hear is a sure way to false hopes, but I have to remind my friend that the extreme of *skepticism*—doubting everything you hear—is an equally dangerous path to follow. In Homer's *Odyssey* the hero, Odysseus, finds his ship in a dangerous place. It is caught between two monsters: the falling rocks of Scylla on one side, and a whirlpool called Charybdis on the other. The hopeful will encounter such dangers and must steer a course between these equally destructive tendencies, avoiding being crushed by the rocks of the doubting skeptics on one hand and being sucked down with a torrent of gullible fools on the other hand.

Roman and Greek myths can illustrate ways in which hopes are sunk. Unfortunately, stories of battered spouses—usually wives—are all too true revelations of the consequences of losing hope. My wife used to run a program for battered (abused) women. One problem she had to frequently deal with was the helpless attitudes of the victims. Why do so many women stay in such terrible situations for so long? A common thought is, "If it's so bad, why don't they just leave?" The reason in many cases is because these women experience a phenomenon that psychologists call *learned helplessness*. What happens in learned helplessness is that a person finds her- or himself in a bad situation and all the efforts directed at alleviating the negative circumstances fail. Consequently, the person becomes *apathetic*, *passive*, *depressed*, and most importantly from the perspective of a battered woman, *gives up* all efforts in trying to get out of the situation and just "takes it." When you lose hope, you're like "the elephant that never forgets." I've heard that when an elephant is initially being trained it is chained such that escape is impossible. The elephant will struggle mightily for a time, but eventually will give up the struggle. Then the elephant can be controlled with little restraint because he or she will not try to escape. The elephant never forgets that escape is impossible. How sad it is that so many people feel like circus animals with no hope of escape, just going on with the same old show. As my wife found with the women she worked with, you have to instill hope in people if you want to not only get people out of bad situations, but also keep them from returning to the same mess.

I've had students in my classes who show signs of learned help-lessness. I've found that in many cases they see themselves as victims but don't realize that their chief victimizers lie in their own minds, by their refusal to let go of the past. There are situations that can crush the hopes of most any person—adulteries, betrayals, losses, failures, etc. But just because someone hurt you once doesn't mean that you have to let that hurt keep hurting you. Just because you failed, doesn't mean you have to keep letting that failure prevent future success. Hope points you forward; get past the pain. Hopelessness chains you to the shores of the past. How can you sail the seas if you can't *let go* of the ropes that hold you to shore? If you refuse to let go of the past, you will eventually become a rotting, decaying hull of a ship once fit for sailing but now only good for ruminating about the things that once were.

> Beside dim waves, the battered ships are dreaming—
> The worn ships, torn ships, with many a draggled mast
> The gray old ships are musing of those creaming
> Waters that weltered in the days long past.
> —from "Old Ships" by Louis Ginsberg

Don't give up the ship! Cut the ropes and sail into a future of marvelous possibilities.

Hope . . .

1. sustains the perseverance of the *courageous*;
2. stimulates people to work for both present and future *justice*;
3. challenges, tests, and sharpens the intellect, opening the mind to new riches of *wisdom*;
4. moves a person to be *temperate* in this world because of the hope of life with God in the next world;
5. directs *faith* forward, sustains it through tough times, ensuring that faith is hallowed, not hollowed;
6. enables *love* to persevere through the difficult times and to work for better times through the belief that love can and will endure forever;

. . . sailing into the future with God.

protects, always trusts, always hopes, always perseveres. Love never fails. ——1 Corinthians 13:4—8

love

AN EXPRESSION OF THE
DIVINE ESSENCE THAT
MANIFESTS ITSELF IN A
TRANSCENDING DEVOTION
TO WHAT IS BEST FOR
SOMEONE

keeps no record of wrongs. Love does not delight in evil but rejoices with the truth. It always

Chapter 8

The Virtue of Violets

The flowers appear on the earth;
the time of singing has come,
and the voice of the turtledove
is heard in our land.

—Song of Sol. 2:12

MY WIFE LOVES TO RECEIVE FLOWERS. I LOVE TO BUY FLOWERS. A GOOD COMbination. My wife's favorites, in keeping with popular opinion, are roses—bright red roses. Roses may be the flower of choice when it comes to symbolizing love for most folks, but I find greater symbolism in a worldwide wildflower: the violet. As a child walking through the meadows or woods, violets with many shadings of their namesake color always caught my eye. As an adult, with the flower of my wife's love blooming in my heart, the beauty of violets has again caught my eye—a beauty that speaks of love. What do I see in these gentle flowers?

The best-known variety of violets are identifiable by their distinctive heart-shaped leaves. People, analogously, are distinguished by what shape their hearts are in. Nothing will shape a heart more than being loved and being able to love. On Valentine's Day we traditionally exchange cards with hearts depicted on them, symbolizing our love for each other. I like this symbolism because the heart represents the *center* around which all else draws life, and the *core* (from the French *coeur,* meaning "heart") issues of life. People whose hearts are shaped by love are the most beautiful flowers in the field of humanity. To love and to be loved is the heart of the matter when it comes to a life well lived.

The violet has five petals on a single stalk, four of which are arrayed in unlike pairs. The fifth has nothing to match it and contains a spur. When I look at the beauty of love, I discern that there are, likewise, five principal features: four of which can be paired together, one that is matchless in its quality. Furthermore, the colors of violets vary, most commonly, from violet to bluish violet, reddish violet, lilac, and white. These diverse shades of the flower symbolize further the different shadings of love's qualities.

The first pair of petals of love I call *intimacy.* Intimacy refers to how well you know someone. One of these petals is called *psychological intimacy*—the degree of mutual self-disclosure: how much people reveal about themselves to each other. This petal has a white color because as white contains all the colors of the visual spectrum, psychological intimacy seeks to embrace and accept all that can be known about another person, from the brightest to the darkest nuances of a person's life. The color white also brings to my mind's eye a knight in shining white armor sitting on a beautiful white horse, the stuff of fairy tales, of romantic heroes, of days gone by. To too many people dreams of finding that special someone with whom they can share their deepest thoughts seems like nothing more than a fictional tale from a bygone era.

When I talk about psychological intimacy in my classes, I can see in the eyes of most of my students that longing, yearning look of "I wish I had somebody like that in my life." The problem in a society that advocates sexual looseness is that a lot of people, in their rush into sexual intimacy, eventually get "dumped" and pay the price in hurt feelings and wounded self-esteem. A number of years ago a lady told me how she decided to pay a surprise visit to her boyfriend's place and was shocked, upon opening his door, to find him engaging in sexual intercourse with another woman. When the other woman asked the guy who was at the door, his reply was "I don't know her." The jilted lady learned a hard lesson: Having sexual intimacy with someone does not mean that psychological intimacy will be involved. She was hurt deeply, and that led to a difficult choice. She could imitate a knight of old and put on the full dressing of armor to protect herself so that "no one can hurt me again." The problem is that as long as the armor is on and the shield is up, no one can get close to her—psychological intimacy is precluded. If, after being wounded, she wants to truly love again, she will have to put down that shield, and take off that armor piece by piece. For people who have been hurt deeply, this will be a long, difficult, and often frightening process. They need a patient, understanding, and gentle partner. But taking off the armor is worth the risk of love. There are those whose hearts are sacred hiding places, in which your deepest secrets are secure, your greatest fears are allayed, and your gravest wounds are healed.

My hope and prayer for you is that you find a friend for your soul like I have found in my beautiful wife.

> . . . You helped refashion the dream of my heart,
> And made me turn eagerly to it;
> There were others who might have (I question that part)—
> But, after all, they didn't do it!
> —from "To a Friend" by Grace Stricker Dawson

The other half of the intimate pair I term *familial intimacy*—the bond of commitment and attachment that people have for one another. The color of this type of love is lilac—a pale, pinkish sort of violet. It is the pinkish tint of violet that makes me think of familial intimacy. A couple of years ago I picked up a used book for my kids about trains. As I was reading the story I mentioned something about "the red caboose" and I was promptly interrupted by my son Karston: "Daddy, the caboose isn't red. It's pink!" Sure enough, on the faded pages of the book, a bright red caboose had faded to pink. That pink caboose reminded me of the commitment people share in familial love: The bright colors of youth fade away with the years, but no matter what, commitment, in the end, like that caboose, keeps people coupled to each other. Young lovers may be drawn to each other in the red heat of passion, but it is the mellow pink of their committed companionship that will keep them together in the long run.

That commitment reminds me of my mother's parents. I can still vividly see them playing cards together on their kitchen table, so enjoying their companionship. Hot love can soon run cold, but the committed "mellowship" of familial love will keep people warm for the rest of their lives. When this type of intimacy joins people together, there is no doubt as to how they will answer the following question:

I would ask of you, my darling,
A question soft and low,
That gives me many a heartache
As the moments come and go.

Your love I know is truthful,
But the truest love grows cold;
It is this that I would ask you:
Will you love me when I'm old?

Life's morn will soon be waning,
And its evening bells be tolled,
But my heart shall know no sadness,
If you'll love me when I'm old.

Down the stream of life together
We are sailing side by side,
Hoping some bright day to anchor
Safe beyond the surging tide.
Today our sky is cloudless,
But the night may clouds unfold;
But, though storms may gather round us,
Will you love me when I'm old?

When my hair shall shade the snowdrift,
And mine eyes shall dimmer grow,
I would lean upon some loved one,
Through the valley as I go.
I would claim of you a promise,
Worth to me a world of gold;
It is only this, my darling,
That you'll love me when I'm old.
　　　　　—from "Will You Love Me When I'm Old?" author unknown

The second pair of love petals I refer to as *passion*. *Psychological passion* refers to the feelings and emotions people have for one another. This type of love is like a bright reddish violet petal—vivid, powerful, and quickly grabbing your attention. People, particularly the so-called experts, will tell you this is not a necessary part of love. There was even a song in the 1980s that contained a line that went something like this: "Love's not a feeling, it's a decision."

I passionately disagree with that. Sure, love requires commitment, but people are committed to all sorts of things they don't necessarily love. I remember playing football and enduring the dreaded summer, two-a-day practices. I was committed to go through the practices, but I definitely did not love them. Sure, love is an exchange of information, but computers do a wonderful job of exchanging all the right sort of info without being in love.

Folks, love is a song that requires words (the knowledge of each other) and a melody (people's feelings and emotions being in tune with each other). When people are genuinely in love with each other, it is impossible to divorce their love lives from their feelings and emotions. Show me a couple "in love" without any positive feelings and emotions for each other, and I'll show you a shell of a relationship that once had life. Show me a Christian with no passion for God, and I'll show you someone who has lost his or her first love. Little great in life has been accomplished without great passion; love that is small is usually revealed by little passion. When your love is deep, your feelings and emotions will be stirred to great depth and great breadth. Lovers will be sensitive to each others' feelings. They will work to overcome negative feelings. They will share with each other the nature that was created in them by the God of the Bible, who is revealed as a passionate God. Genuine love will bring up all sorts of feelings and emotions. Experiencing them, learning from them, and using them to express your love to your loved ones, neighbors, and God is part of the wonderful language of love. Don't be dumb. Speak this multifaceted language.

How do I love thee? Let me count the ways.
I love thee to the depth and breadth and height
My soul can reach, when feeling out of sight
For the ends of Being and ideal Grace.
I love thee to the level of every day's
Most quiet need; by sun and candle-light
I love thee freely, as men strive for Right;
I love thee purely, as they turn from Praise.
I love thee with the passion put to use
In my old griefs, and with my childhood's faith.
I love thee with a love I seemed to lose
With my lost saints,—I love thee with the breath,
Smiles, tears, of all my life!—and, if God choose,
I shall love thee better after death.
—from "How Do I Love Thee? Let Me Count the Ways"
by Elizabeth Barrett Browning

The second petal of passion is *physical* passion—how lovers show their love through their bodies. When the expression "making love" is said, the first thought is usually of sexual activity. That's why I give this petal of the violet a violet color: It's the first color you typically think of when thinking of a violet. But just as violets encompass many different shadings of colors, so too physical passion is varied in its expression. For example, when you look at people in love you easily find it in their body language. Lovers love to look in each others' eyes. When gazes are averted, something is usually wrong with the love life. Lovers can be found unpretentiously holding hands, kissing, and hugging. They like being physically close to each other because they are psychologically close to one another.

Love, of course, given the right type of relationship—it's called *marriage*—can be expressed sexually. Plato, in his *Symposium,* distinguished between *profane* and *sacred* love. *Profane* love is concerned with the body, getting physical pleasure, and emphasizes what you can do for me. *Sacred* love is concerned with the soul, the pleasure of knowing someone, and emphasizes what I can do for you. When two people love each other with a sacred love, their sexuality becomes a gift of God, an expression of their commitment to each other, and a sign of their unity. This love, in the sight of God, causes two people to "become one flesh" (Gen. 2:24). Why are people in such a hurry to tear apart this sacred bond? Don't they realize the significance of joining yourself to another?

> The fountains mingle with the river,
> And the rivers with the ocean;
> The winds of heaven mix forever,
> With a sweet emotion;
> Nothing in the world is single;
> All things by a law divine
> In one another's being mingle:—
> Why not I with thine?
>
> See! the mountains kiss high heaven,
> And the waves clasp one another;
> No sister flower would be forgiven
> If it disdained its brother;
> And the sunlight clasps the earth,
> And the moonbeams kiss the sea:—
> What are all these kissings worth,
> If thou not kiss not me?
> —from "Love's Philosophy" by Percy Bysshe Shelley

Sacredly kiss your loved one while you embrace the love of God.
God is found prominently in the fifth, unmatched petal—the
spiritual quality of love. I see the color blue in this sacred petal. Love
is found in self-disclosure, commitment, affection, and physical expression, but the quintessential quality of love is spurred by the
nature of God. This spiritual quality seeks what is best for someone
with no expectation of a return. It is making a gift out of your love
just as God made a gift to the human race out of His own Son. How
well do you express this kind of love? Consider the following:

If you sit down at set of sun
And count the acts that you have done,
And counting find
One self-denying deed, one word
That eased the heart of him who heard;
One glance most kind,
That felt like sunshine where it went—
Then you may count that day well spent.

But if, through all the livelong day,
You're cheered no heart, by yea or nay—
If, through it all
You've nothing done that you can trace
That brought the sunshine to one face;
No act most small
That helped some soul and nothing cost—
Then count that day as worse than lost.
—from "Count That Day Lost" by George Eliot

Spiritual love is a gift that intends the best for another. The best-
intended acts, however, can go wrong. When my wife and I were
making preparations for our wedding reception, I was warned by
the lady baking the wedding cake not to lean against the table. Curious as to her reason, I asked her why. She then related the following story:

Earlier that summer, another couple held a reception in the same
room, with a long reception line dutifully forming in front of the
couple standing by the wedding cake. The groom, tiring a bit, began to lean against the table. Unfortunately, he put a bit too much
weight on the table, and it collapsed. The groom fell to the floor, the
cake catapulted into the air, part of it landing on the groom, another

part rolling past the reception line. The bride, acting as if nothing had happened, continued to shake hands with well-wishers with nary a glance at either her dazed and fallen, cake-crowned groom or the rolling cake! Now, that is a lot like love. We sometimes fall down and make a mess out of things, but our lover, like that bride, overlooks the messes. True love forgives the messes lovers make. If you forfeit forgiveness, you will forget how to love. Love does not demand that the other be perfect, rather by extending the freedom that comes with forgiveness, love is less likely to become messed up.

On the other hand, maybe the bride was too composed, too ignorant. When love messes up, there is a time for intervention, not ignorance, in order to clear matters up. But it is an intervention that supports the other, not kicks the one who is down. Love builds up, not tears down. The wisdom of loving is knowing when to build and when to refrain from such efforts; when to speak and when to keep silent (Eccl. 3:1–8). No matter what the case may be, the spiritual nature of love directs a person to hope, think, and work for the best for another.

> There is so much good in the worst of us,
> And so much bad in the best of us,
> That it ill behaves any of us,
> To find fault with the rest of us.
> —from "Charity," author unknown

Gems of Love

> See, I lay a stone in Zion, a tested stone, a precious cornerstone for a sure foundation; the one who trusts will never be dismayed. (Isa. 28:16)

In 1477, Maximillian of Austria placed a diamond ring on the third finger of the left hand of Mary of Burgundy to seal their marriage vows. Ancient wisdom had decreed that the third finger was directly connected to the heart by the vein of love. Since that time this ritual has been repeated countless times by lovers, indelibly connecting the diamond with love. But, what is it about diamonds that supposedly symbolize love? I wanted to find out, so I arranged an interview with a jewelry store owner who was intimately acquainted with the diamond business. As he told me the story of diamonds, from beginning to end (often ending up on a finger!),

I found that diamonds, indeed, do have a wonderful story to tell about love.

Rough diamonds, dull and opaque, are mined from the earth. Much work is needed before a precious gem is developed. The beginning of love is also only a rough approximation of what is possible. Much work will be needed to bring into reality the possibilities. A diamond cutter will carefully study the rough diamond, sometimes for years, before making the first, most important cleave of the rock according to the unique grain of the particular diamond. Couples, through time, study the unfolding of their relationship: Is it just a good friendship, or can it be more? After enough consideration a decision must be reached: Should we marry or not?

Next will come the shaping process, as the diamond begins to take a particular shape, such as an oval, emerald, marquise, etc. Then the diamond cutter will skillfully make little cuts designed to enhance the ability of the gem to reflect and refract light. As I look back at my marriage to Kathleen, I enjoy seeing how our relationship has grown in beauty through the years. We have both learned much about each other, and this has shaped a beautiful marriage. Furthermore, I have learned that the greatest acts of love are the little things: the kind words, the wink of an eye, a pat on the back. Great love will be found when there are many "little" acts of love.

Finally, the final polishing with diamond dust mixed with olive oil, will craft the diamond into a beautiful gem. About half of the total weight of the rough diamond is lost in the process. Lovers polish one another through their interactions. It is important to note that friction is necessary in this process. Sometimes being "rubbed the wrong way" by another is the right way to remove impediments to a greater love. The cutting, shaping, and polishing remove a lot of the original rough diamond, and the dynamic forces at work between lovers will remove a lot that will inhibit the loveliness of their relationship.

The finished product will go to a diamond dealer who will determine its value based on its cut, color, clarity, and carat. The cut of the diamond determines its shape. The shape of a couple's love for each other is determined by how they choose to "cut" their interactions. The more transparent the color of a diamond, the more valuable it is. The more transparent—open and honest— a couple is with each other, the more precious their love. Clarity refers to the degree of "inclusions"—fractures, impurities, etc.—in a diamond; the more flawless the diamond, the better the value. As couples work to reduce the imperfections in their relationship, so too their relationship grows in value. The carat of the diamond is its weight; generally, the heavier, the more valuable. The greater the weight of a relationship—the more the relationship becomes life's priority—the more precious it is. This was succinctly summarized in Luke 12:34 by Jesus Christ: "For where your treasure is, there will your heart be also."

One of the most remarkable aspects of the diamond business is how the diamonds are acquired from diamond cutters. A price is negotiated for the gem, and then the diamond is handed over to the diamond broker. No written contracts are drawn up and signed, no money immediately exchanges hands. What is unique about those who trade in diamonds is that their word is their bond once an agreement is made. I asked the jewelry store owner, "What would happen if either partner in the deal reneged on the agreement?" He told me that if that ever happened, the guilty partner would be banished from the diamond business and would lose his or her occupation in that business throughout the world. Trading in the diamond business is based on absolute trust. Likewise, love is founded on trust. The weaker the trust in a relationship, the more superficial the love. Christians who have little trust that the Bible is God's revelation to humanity have small love for God. How can you love someone you can't trust? But how you can feel secure in your love when you can trust in that special someone. What comfort, what safety, what contentment there is when your heart securely rests in *true* love.

> Oh, the comfort—the inexpressible comfort of feeling safe with a person,
> Having neither to weigh thoughts,
> Nor measure words—but pouring them
> All right out—just as they are—
> Chaff and grain together—
> Certain that a faithful hand will
> Take and sift them—
> Keep what is worth keeping—
> And with the breath of kindness
> Blow the rest away.
> —from "Friendship" by Dinah Maria Mulock Craik

THE ART OF VIRTUE

Faded Flowers

> The grass withers, the flower fades, but the word of our God will stand forever. (Isa. 40:8)

I was once at a party and met a man with whom I struck up a conversation. Eventually our conversation made its way to the topic of marriage and my acquaintance began sharing with me about his failed marriage and divorce. He tried to sum it all up by stating, "We just weren't growing together." I felt a sense of sadness yet skepticism about that statement. Sadness, because when the flower of love fades much beauty is lost. I love giving pretty bouquets to my wife, but I must admit I always feel a tinge of sadness whenever I see the dried flowers in the garbage can. Skepticism, because I didn't truly accept his explanation—it was too convenient, too antiseptic, too nice, too easy of an excuse to dismiss a relationship that at one time was to be "until death we depart." No, if it's so easy to explain away love, then you're either in denial or it was probably never really the fullness of love in the first place. Never really the fullness of love? Again, violets prove instructive in addressing that question.

During a conversation with a florist, I asked her the following question: "If you keep violets alive, will they inevitably bloom in their colorful petals?"

She responded "No, violets produce lots of leaves, and if you don't prune them back, not enough sunlight will get to the center of the plant and colorful petals will not show forth." Her answer prompted me to think about one way people are confused about love: relationships that are the "right flower" but fail to blossom into the fullness of love. In other words, there are *positive interpersonal qualities* that may grow into the fullness of love, but in and of themselves, they are not love. I think, especially, of attraction, attachment, and liking in this regard.

Attraction is the drawing of people together. It can be based on a person's looks, shared beliefs, or a charming attitude. These qualities may draw you to a person and might be an early prelude to a loving relationship. But remember, looking good does not mean that a person *is* good, commonality of opinion does not mean unity of love, and charm can be deceptive—if not even a cover-up for exploitive intents.

Attachment is a connection, what keeps people together. This may be a sign of devotion to another or an expression of dependency, an unwillingness to let go, a symptom of a parasitic relationship.

Liking is a preference for someone you enjoy being with. People in love will like each other's company, but liking a person does not mean that you're in love with her or him. Liking offers good growth potential for the greater fullness of loving, and therefore the line between the two may be difficult to see and confusing. That's why you have probably found yourself at some point in your life hearing or saying, "I really like you as a friend, but . . ." Getting colorful petals takes pruning and light. When you find yourself attracted, attached, and/or liking another person, you must cut back (not cut totally off) those relationships that through enlightenment you realize cannot grow into the fullness of the love of marriage.

There are many varieties and hybrids of violets. There are also plants that are sometimes mistaken for violets. Purple passion, for example, can show the same colors as violets but is a different species of plant. Pansies may have petals in the shape and colors of violets, but although of the same genus as violets, they are also a different species. Purple passion and pansies could effectively masquerade as violets for a great many folks. Unfortunately, a lot of people are fooled by relationships that are only *masquerades* of love, another way people can be confused about love.

Infatuation is a strong attraction to the superficial qualities of someone who does not return those sentiments. I once had a friend who was infatuated with a particular woman. He once said to me, "She's so perfect I can't even imagine her going to the bathroom." Talk about superficial! The objects of an infatuation are usually unavailable sources of admiration, whereas lovers always freely avail themselves of one another.

Jealousy is wanting to keep from others what you have. A student once told me that her boyfriend "loved" her so much that he would rarely let her out of his sight, and when he would, he'd ask many questions about what she did when she wasn't in his presence. I told her that his behavior wasn't loving, because his actions were rooted in insecurity. Love is rooted in security. Jealous people treat their supposed loved ones as possessions. When someone truly loves you, you are free to choose to love that person back.

Lust seeks after temporary self-centered pleasure, with the other person being simply an object for pleasure. True love desires the eternal pleasure of knowing another person. I've known many guys who loved to brag about their sexual conquests. I've also met many women who have been the victims of such predators. And I've felt the hurt that lingers when someone who has been treated like royalty for a while is then thrown out on the streets like they're worth nothing at all.

One of the most deceptive masquerades of love is *narcissistic manipulation*. Narcissists have an excessive interest in themselves. When narcissists are "in love," what they love is not the other person, but rather their image of an ideal person projected on that person. Narcissists are preoccupied with how closely others match up to their ideal images, not with the genuine welfare of the other person. A woman once treated me like I was a knight on a white horse. It was very flattering. However, I began to find out that I could never come down from that steed. It's impossible to stay on that horse forever; everybody has flaws. "But I thought you were perfect," is the thought of the narcissist. Once you destroy the image of perfection in the mind of a narcissist, the narcissist will be unable to ever show you the affection and care that he or she once did. Beware of those who idolize you; the true source of admiration lies within the idols of the narcissists' minds.

For violets to flourish they need the proper amount of sunlight, the necessary quantity of water, and nutritious soil. Deprive violets of any of these and the plants will surely die. There are three human attributes that will surely *kill* the flower of love.

Pride is like a lack of water—dry, arid arrogance—in which a lofty opinion of self leads to looking down on others. When you genuinely love someone you will look up to that person in respect and admiration. For prideful people, concern for others is replaced by contempt, humility is superseded by haughtiness, and serving others is secondary to self-serving ways. True love is captured in a line from Adelaide Anne Procter's poem "Fidelis":

Where Love has once breathed, Pride dieth;

Hatred is an inner darkness—a fixation on dark, evil thoughts toward others that blots out the life-giving sunlight to love. When people hate, they have a strong ill will and dislike for others. Their greatest joy in life comes from when bad things happen to the objects of their hatred. Hateful people work to tear down the lives of others. Love thinks the best of others, rejoices when good happens in their lives, and works to build up the lives of others. The curious thing about loving relationships is that when they go wrong, they easily can turn into hateful relationships. How much animosity divorced people can direct at the one they once loved! Even the devil was once the angel of light. Once you travel down the road of the darkness of hate, it's very hard to love again. Just ask Darth Vader of *Stars Wars* fame!

The proper soil for love to grow in is unselfishness. People who are *self-centered*, always thinking of themselves first, and can't defer to the desires of others at times, are not able to provide the suitable soil for love to develop. However, just because you provide the right soil does not mean that your plant will grow. To illustrate, my wife once said to me, "You're never really in love until you're loved." At first I kind of recoiled from this statement. Being a rather idealistic sort of guy, I thought that if you loved anybody enough she or he would certainly love you. But, as I began to consider the frustrated spouses who give their lives wholeheartedly toward their partners only to be rejected time after time after time, as I thought of the distraught adoptive parents who find that their adoptive child never really accepts their love, I came to the conclusion that love is not a one-way street. It takes unselfishness on the part of *both* partners if there is to be a loving relationship. Love is not, however, a magic pill that will automatically change the lives of others—that's witchcraft. Love is the most powerful force in the universe, but it only works when people are not forced to respond to it. Jesus Christ offered His life as a loving sacrifice for the sins of the world. God does not, however, force any person to accept that gift. What is freely given must be freely responded to. Selfishness will prevent the growth of love, but unselfishness does not guarantee that love will grow either.

It hurts not to be loved. I've been there. I've been rejected in love. So what do you do when the love that once was is gone, the love that you once hoped for never appears, the relationship that you're in now falls so short of what it could be? There's one more story about violets that I'd like to share with you in this regard. I've been told that the fragrance of violets is sweeter once they've been crushed. I was crushed in love once. But then Kathleen came into my life and accepted me for who I am: a work in progress. I felt like such a failure at love when we first married that when Kathleen said to me, "What did I ever do to deserve you?" I responded by saying, "I don't know, but I'm sure God has forgiven you by now!"

As I sit here writing this chapter, our eighth wedding anniversary is getting close. I am amazed at how fantastic our marriage is, how much Kathleen loves me—how sweet the fragrance of love is after it once was crushed. Don't ever give up on love! I know for a fact that God can "restore for you the years that the locust has eaten. . . ." (Joel 2:25). He has done that for me; He can do it for you!

> The night has a thousand eyes,
> The day but one;
> Yet the light of the bright world dies
> With the dying sun.
> The mind has a thousand eyes,
> And the heart but one;
> Yet the light of a whole life dies
> When it's love is done.
>
> —from "Light" by Francis W. Bourdillon

Love . . .

1. infuses *courage* with goodness and inspires people to be courageous;
2. harmonizes *justice* as rightness is kissed by goodness, just principles are embraced by what is most principal, and just desserts go hand-in-hand with undeserved mercy;
3. imparts the qualities of cherishing, treasuring, and longing for to those who search for *wisdom*, especially the riches of the only wise God;
4. cleanses a *temperate* person of those vices that would pollute the purity of true love;
5. serves as the greatest source of *faith* and the greatest means of practicing that faith;
6. projects into another's *hopes* and reveals that, because of God's love, the darkness of death dissipates in the light of the hope of salvation;

. . . the pure, beautiful, and precious commitment to the good of others, the very nature of God.